Retirement

By Design

How To Avoid Running Out of Money
and Create the Income You Need,
To Live the Way You Want!

Elisabeth M. Dawson

ISBN: 978-0-578-27874-2

SPECIAL DISCLAIMER:

The contents of this book are meant to be informational only. You should consult your legal, tax, and financial advisor before implementing any ideas suggested herein. Ms. Dawson is held harmless for any actions or inactions individuals may take or not take because of the information in this book. Ms. Dawson is not acting as a fiduciary in her capacity as author of this work. Copia Wealth Management and Insurance Services and Copia Wealth Management Advisors, Inc. also waves any liability for publishing this work.

"*Retirement By Design* is an enjoyable and educational read on how to safeguard your retirement plan. Elisabeth explains effective strategies for accumulating savings, the pluses, and the minuses in a simple and logical manner. This book is a must-read for people who are concerned with safeguarding their retirement and don't want to worry about outliving their income."

-Salvatore Petruzzella, CLU, ChFC, Industry Expert

"Elisabeth shares the keys to a successful retirement but more importantly, she guides you through the financial structure you need to make it a reality. She does an incredible job of providing the necessary tools for long-term financial security. Elisabeth's knowledge and experience are top-notch. She identifies the pitfalls many people face and outlines how to avoid them. I've seen what she can do, and her financial process is the whole package."

-Mike Steranka, Author, Speaker, and Retirement Specialist

"Once again Elisabeth Dawson has hit a home run! As one of the top financial advisors in the country, she has the unique ability to make something very complex, and easy to understand. For some, this book will be a life changer, for some, this book will be a lifesaver!"

-Brian Gengler, President of First Income Advisors

"*Retirement by Design* is yet another example of Elisabeth's thought leadership in the financial planning world. The book is a no-nonsense guide to better financial outcomes using a coordinated and comprehensive approach to all aspects of financial planning. Elisabeth lays out how to steward your day-to-day and year-to-year life to find your desired outcome, even with all the twists and turns that this world has to offer. Enjoy the read and implement!"

-Joe Strazzeri, Counselor and Attorney at Law

Table of Contents

Introduction

I am Elisabeth Dawson and I am on a mission to help as many people as possible in this world achieve greatness in their financial lives.

For over 24 years, I've been helping clients like you experience freedom and hope around money.

In that time, without question, the number one concern people express to me, is not having enough money to retire or the fear of running out of money in retirement.

Are you feeling this fear too right now?

If so, I have good news and bad news for you.

The bad news is that there's an entire industry full of extremely well-paid people whose entire job is to sell you a bunch of misconceptions about your retirement so that they can feed at your trough. This is the "retirement industry" promulgated by Wall Street. In all likelihood, you've already fallen for several of these misconceptions, and you may be following the dictates of their plan... a plan that leads to their profit and your peril.

The good news is... there's an antidote to these lies and misconceptions. *And you're holding it in your hands!*

This book is packed with the information you need to take back your retirement from the profiteers who have a vested interest in keeping you dependent on them... and to design your retirement on your terms.

In this book, you will learn:

- The top 5 **enemies** of your abundant retirement and how to combat them
- The massive expense **1-in-5 retirees** forget about until it's too late... will you be one of them?
- The insanely important retirement step that only 2% of people handle... (failing to do this could cause years of grief for your entire family)
- How inflation will **kill your retirement** if you don't take this one counterintuitive but easy action...
- What is the #1 investment you should make now to enjoy an **abundant retirement?**
- How NOT to run out of money in retirement
- How to **reclaim $30,000+ a year** in money you're currently throwing away unnecessarily in tax mistakes and other "phantom" expenses.

Millions of people think, "It can wait. I'm young and I have plenty of time to catch up."

I'm going to be straight with you:

It cannot wait.

Every year you're not finding money as I teach you how to do in this book...

And every year you're not investing that money as I explain...

Is a year you're not gaining compound returns that snowball into your own abundant retirement.

There is simply no way to design the retirement you want without the benefit of those compound returns.

Small differences today add up to millions of dollars in your retirement as the snowball of wealth builds on itself.

Even waiting one year could significantly diminish your retirement.

It happens all the time...

30-year-olds pay for money mistakes they made in their 20s...

40-year-olds pay for money mistakes they made in their 30s...

50-year-olds pay for money mistakes they made in their 40s...

Given how often I've seen these sad cases in my 24 years as a professional financial advisor, I have one simple question for you:

In ten years, do you want to be paying for money mistakes you're making today?

I assume your answer is "Heck No!"

That's why I've written my second book, **Retirement by Design,** for you.

Like the title says, this book will help you **design** your current and future financial reality so that your future self is going to **bring out champagne and toast you!**

"Where were you 10 years ago?" clients often ask me once we've designed their retirement easefully.

I respectfully say, "I was here the entire time, you just weren't ready for me yet."

The fact that you're holding this book in your hands shows that you're ready.

Let's begin.

Chapter 1

The Dark Side of Traditional Financial Planning

The 1980s marked a dramatic shift in funding the retirement of millions of Americans—a shift that is probably impacting you today in ways you don't realize.

Up until that time, company pensions were common and most people relied on the promise of lifetime income in exchange for their years of loyal service to an employer. Previous generations saw many individuals working for one employer throughout the majority of their careers. In turn, employees were guaranteed a comfortable pension upon their retirement as a reward for their decades of service. Such pensions were often generous and continued to pay out until the passing of the former employee.

The 1980s brought the introduction of employer retirement plans such as 401(k)s, 403(b)s, TSPs, 457 plans, and other savings plans. This placed the fiscal responsibility of preparing for retirement on the individual. With these new retirement savings plans, large corporations and municipalities were able to relieve themselves of the financial burden of funding their workers' retirement years. As a result, many pensions were frozen, shut down, or no longer available for future generations of workers.

Today, traditional pensions in the US have almost disappeared completely. In fact, the majority of privately owned companies today no longer offer pension options to their employees. For those older pension plans still in existence, there is a growing number of plans that face bankruptcy due to the inability to sustain guaranteed payouts to workers who have earned them.

States are beginning to minimize what income benefits they will provide for employees who have earned a lifetime pension income. For the first time ever, big pension companies are paying out a lump sum and letting you figure out how to make your money last into retirement. While frightening to imagine, too many working individuals today may not yet grasp the resulting burden poised to land squarely on their shoulders, appointing them as the sole provider of their own financial security throughout their retirement years.

As a nation, we are faced with a crisis we don't want to deal with and are scared to death to even talk about! The fear of running out of money in retirement is mounting. This is why the majority of people approaching retirement are beginning to question whether they will be able to stop working. It's time to hit the eject button and escape from this wild rollercoaster ride before it loses control and jumps the tracks. Don't wait until it's a matter of life and death. You need to act now and map out how you want things to go.

Are you ready to follow a path to create a successful financial future for yourself or are you just going to take your chances when you get there? Do you want to wake up one day and realize you are left with whatever remains after raising children, paying for college and weddings, etc.? After working hard for so many years, imagine wondering what is left for you to live the life you wanted for the rest of your years.

It's a crisis: to allow your future to fall victim, as you work to satisfy today's demands and meet the needs of everyone around you. Who will come to your rescue? Do you think the government or your kids will supply the income you need to live? Will they ensure you can keep up with inflation, health care, prescriptions, home maintenance, travel, and anything else that pops up in your future?

The most important thing to recognize is that you are the only one who will save, plan for and protect your financial future. That is why income is such an incredibly important topic: when you control your income, you control what your reality will look like in retirement.

People who save a large amount in retirement accounts can be lulled into a false sense of security. They see a $1-$2 million account balance and assume there's no way they could have a problem in retirement. The truth is, taxes and inflation are going to take a huge bite out of that balance. Of course, without a detailed income plan, they may not realize the reality of the situation until it's far too late. That is how funding retirement has become such a crisis for so many people.

You've worked hard to accumulate assets, savings, and investments over your working years. You've done a great job! Understand, though, the accumulation phase of building wealth is generally not the hardest part. Sure, you may face some hiccups getting started or struggle with procrastination, but once you're set up and you're consistent, you've got it. I've even been told that accumulating a 401(k) or other employer retirement plan was easy. The problem becomes how to create the income you'll need from the money you've saved. Most people don't know where to start or what their options are.

It's All Up to You (Or Is It?)

Although the burden of saving and planning for retirement rests on your shoulders, I have good news: you don't have to do it alone.

The right financial professional will understand how every aspect of your financial life interacts and understand your trajectory. He or she will see potential problems before they occur and help you develop a plan accordingly.

Our Wealth by Design team specializes in exactly such an approach. We help you design a personalized approach to wealth creation, all centered around your unique wish list. We show you how to get from where you are now, to a financial reality you may have dreamed of but perhaps thought was out of your reach. You can achieve all of this with a structured and systematic approach tailored to your desires for your lifetime, and beyond. Perhaps most important, we show you how to avoid some of the most common and devastating financial missteps.

Understand that the majority of people only have access to the limited information that is offered to consumers. Do you have the means to obtain information that is published for professionals? Perhaps you do but, my guess is, probably not.

Please don't think that I am minimizing what you have accomplished. You are doing the very best you can, with the information you have at your disposal. However, there is a reason that you are reading this book. You are questioning the knowledge that's available at your fingertips. You are questioning the information that has been offered to you by your current financial professional.

I would venture to guess that the material we will cover here is new to you and your current stock broker or advisor has never said any of this to you before. Why? They want you to continue trying to accumulate your assets and keep your money in the market so they can continue making money, whether you do or not. Ultimately, it doesn't matter to them whether you are making money. Even if you are in a down or depressed market, you are still stuck paying fees and expenses that benefit their bottom line. How is that fair? Quite frankly, it's not.

You see, there is a professional for everything and, in every profession, there are good and bad professionals within the industry. I don't believe it's right for these types of "advisors" to take advantage of people's vulnerabilities and prioritize commissions over clients' best interests. That is why I believe in talking about this and standing up for people like you.

You need a great professional fiduciary who specializes in retirement income distribution planning. This is critical because your retirement reality will depend on it. If you are working with an advisor who has never discussed what your guaranteed income distribution will look like, either today or in the future, then you have the wrong financial professional.

This is very different from a stock broker helping you invest in the market and accumulate; he or she doesn't know where to take it from there. You probably don't know where to take it from there, which is why you're here. You need a true comprehensive fiduciary financial advisor who has the expertise to guarantee your future income, no matter what happens to the economy or the stock market. You need to ensure your monthly income will keep coming in – no matter what. Too many people don't know to do this and that is why we, as a society, have a major problem.

Income Solves the Problem!

We all remember the market correction in 2008 and you may have heard personal stories about the devastation it caused. Millions of people watched their dreams for retirement go down the drain as they lost 50-65% of their portfolio or more. These people were no different from you and me. They worked hard, and tried to do everything right, yet watched helplessly as their long-awaited retirement evaporated right in front of their eyes.

What would happen if you were to lose 50-65% or more, on your portfolio today? Could you retire as planned? If you're already retired, could you stay retired if you lost half of your money? I'm guessing probably not. What if you have a health event and you don't have enough monthly income to cover it? What if your parent or child has a health event? Many of us would do anything to help a loved one, but what impact will that have on our own future? How would your personal retirement income suffer? If you don't have reliable income then you can't provide effective support in any of these situations.

These scenarios are real for too many people: heartbreaking stories happening to individuals across the country. At some point, we need to wake up and take action if we have any hope to create a better future for ourselves and our loved ones.

Chapter 2

The Biggest Financial Fraud Revealed

With the shift from traditional company pensions to individuals funding their own retirement, Wall Street had to become creative to lure hard-working individuals to start putting money into the market to work on their retirement.

You see, prior to the 1980s (for the last 300 years or so), people would purchase whole life insurance. They would purchase these policies when a couple got married or a baby was born to cover the main breadwinner's income, thus protecting the financial security of the spouse and children at home. The cash values in these policies would grow and when it came to retirement, the consumer would turn the cash accumulation into a supplemental income annuity stream at retirement age.

Big business, Wall Street, and the insurance industry all knew this. Corporations would target the money people paid for whole life insurance premiums and tell consumers to put it away for themselves in their new retirement plan (called the 401K) offered at work. With the risk of saving for retirement on the shoulders of the worker, they were told, "Buy term life insurance instead and invest the difference of what you have been putting into your whole life insurance policies." Then when you get to retirement, you won't need life insurance anyway. The objective of protecting the American family first disappeared the day Americans bought into this.

This was an effective tactic to get more money into Wall Street, while shifting the risk and responsibility of retirement savings onto the consumer. Years later, when the consumer truly needed the death benefit of their life insurance, it had expired. After years of paying into a term life insurance policy, their surviving spouse and children were left without income, liquidity, or resources to take care of what they needed to continue to live. The money they did have was all in IRAs, facing high taxes and market volatility. Does this sound familiar? Is this you today?

How well do you understand Wall Street?

Wall Street monetizes the fact that most Americans don't understand how the stock market works. The majority of investors buy stocks, mutual funds, and other traded investments when all the Wall Street professionals have sold out months, if not years, ago.

They watch you take the hit and then profit on your losses when they buy them again at a discount. You see, Wall Street runs on money supplied by uneducated investors.

The public is told that the best way to get ahead is to invest and that's how to build wealth. "Invest in the stock market, be speculative, and don't worry: you'll make lots of money because investing provides the highest returns over time to outpace inflation." Of course, what you're investing in will ultimately determine your financial success. The truth is, you are riding out every economic hiccup, paying ridiculous management fees, and enduring incredible risk, with little to no return. After all, who do you think is most hurt by volatility in the markets? The bankers and stockbrokers on Wall Street? Or is it you: individual investors who risk their hard-earned money, in an effort to get ahead and save for retirement? How is this helping you achieve your dreams for retirement?

Ok, so why do people continue to place their trust in these portfolio managers? It's simple: a lack of knowledge, a lack of confidence, and a lack of options. Because that's what everyone tells you to do. Right?

Aren't the big retail investment houses supposed to be looking out for you? No, they aren't. They are looking out for themselves. They can't get the average consumer out of the way of the fatal fluctuation of a market crash or major correction. They need you to be the ones that take that hit, not them. They protect their own paycheck, bottom line, and balance sheet. You are merely a cog in the wheel of Wall Street's success... and that's not your fault! You are busy working, raising a family, and living your life. You shouldn't be required to use every spare moment learning the ins and outs of Wall Street in order to build wealth and achieve a financially secure future. Or should you?

When it comes to investing, we've all heard that you should buy low and sell high. That is what the top 2% of investors do: they stick to the process, don't get hung up on emotions, and follow the market every day. Yet, most money managers are not doing this at all! They are telling you to ride out the market and wait for it to bounce back. Why? Because they are collecting a commission or fee the whole time!

"Stay in the market, stay the course, the market will come back, it has to." I'm sure you have heard people say this before, whenever the market corrects and investors lose money.

First of all, the very nature of the stock market is that it provides no guarantees. You are not guaranteed to make money and, in fact, many investors ultimately lose money. You could say, the stock market is a form of legalized gambling for the not-so-faint of heart.

However, what you need to consider is how long will it take for you to recover from your investment losses. Most people don't have time to waste trying to regain maximum declines. Will it take five years? Ten years? Will your investments ever return to their highs? Once they return, will they have the same buying power they lost all those years ago when they initially took the hit?

I have seen portfolio positions that have never recovered since even before the year 2000. Sure, eventually you can recover some of your losses from a market downturn but the question is, what are you giving up in return? What could your money have been doing for you while you were stuck waiting to regain what you had? Not to mention, do you really feel in control of your money as you sit there hoping stocks will return to their peak? Of course not. At that point, you are helpless and at the mercy of forces beyond your control.

Society has created the narrative that by putting money in your employer's retirement savings plan, you're doing everything you need to prepare for your retirement. However, these retirement plans are invested in the stock market and are vulnerable to all of the risk and volatility that entails. The truth is, most individuals who are diligently putting money into such qualified savings plans as their only preparation for retirement, don't understand their investment portfolio, the fees they're paying, or even how the stock market works.

Do you see the problem here?

Why has society directed your entire focus to this one path? Where have the real fundamentals in financial planning gone? Where is the foundation of protection we need to establish for our families? Everyone deserves to enjoy life's momentous occasions such as births, marriages, and buying a home. Perhaps you're planning for a child's wedding or the anticipation of your first grandchild. How can we accomplish these things and still accumulate liquid savings to cover emergency expenses and maintenance costs? Not to mention, how can we protect our family from unexpected life events, such as if you or your spouse pass away suddenly?

If liquid savings and emergency funds take a back seat to investing, what happens when you need new tires, or brakes, for your car? Instead of planning, budgeting, and having some money for your "real life" needs, you end up doing exactly what the banks and financial institutions promote: use credit cards to help you survive all those everyday life expenses that pop up. You think you're doing everything right, but instead of creating wealth for yourself and your family, you end up creating wealth for the credit card companies and big businesses on Wall Street.

Now, don't get me wrong, I love Wall Street, but it's far from perfect and the money you have invested there must never have any impact on the monthly income sources that you depend on when you're finally in retirement. If you want to accomplish your goals and live the life you've imagined, both today and in retirement, Wall Street is not the only place to make it happen.

I see so many people today putting all their eggs in "speculative" investments that are such high risk. Speculative investments should only be for extra money – not the foundation of your financial plan. For the money you depend on to live your life, look elsewhere. There's simply too much at risk.

I ask this question to every client that I meet with: "How well do you understand Wall Street?"

I've been in the financial services industry for over 23 years and I've never had anyone claim that they fully understand. The majority of people truly do not understand Wall Street, even though they have been told they should invest in it. This is the reason so many investors are left wondering why their account seems to lose value more quickly and recover more slowly than the overall market.

To have any hope of getting ahead, you have to demand that your assets work harder for you, in environments where they can make more money with the least amount of fees, costs, and expenses. Making this conscious decision will help your assets perform better, reduce any undue risk, and avoid financial pitfalls along the way.

Recover thousands of dollars and put this wasted money to work for your retirement. Every month you wait is lost wealth.

Get started now with your FREE Wealth Recovery Checklist: www.RetirementByDesignBook.com/checklist

---

Chapter 3

The Most Dangerous Risk That Can Derail Your Dream Retirement

There is no debating it: you absolutely must understand the market risk within your investments. There is no way around it and no excuse for overlooking it. Why do I say this? Simply put: too much is at stake. You've put in the work, sacrificed your time, earned the money, and invested it, believing it will grow and provide for your future. Yet, you don't really understand what you have.

The Risk You Don't Realize You're Taking Right Now!

How much risk is embedded within your retirement savings plan? Most people can't really answer this question. Why is that? Because, again, most people don't understand the details of their investments.

That's not the problem. In fact, as we've discussed, the majority of people don't have an in-depth understanding of the stocks, bonds, and other investments they have. The problem is, too many people don't realize the risk their investments carry. This means they are making plans for the future based on incomplete and potentially inaccurate information. I'm confident you can see how this will lead to failure and disappointment, more often than not.

We often see new clients come to us with risk ratios (correlated to the market) of 55% or 60%, in situations where this simply doesn't make sense based on the person's age, goals, income needs, and other factors. This means that if the market goes down by 50%, the potential losses associated with their investment options could be as high as 55% or more. This is often one reason investors have no idea why their account values drop even further than the market when a major correction occurs.

I have even seen a client with a loss ratio exceeding 80% who had no idea their risk exposure was anywhere near that level. This is frightening! It's a shame and another reason why it's important to understand the type of financial professional you are working with.

So many money managers and stockbrokers try to beat the market while they collect a commission or a fee on your hard-earned dollars. The fact is, they have no skin in the game: they will get paid regardless of market performance and generally won't be held accountable if your portfolio tanks in value. In fact, statistics show that once you net out asset management fees, less than 20% of asset managers meet or exceed the performance of the S&P 500.[1] Brokers and money managers will tell you all about the average rates of returns. Very few of them will explain the potential for loss embedded in your portfolio.

Often, once people find out the extent of the market risk embedded in their portfolio, they are shocked. They feel misled and tell me they thought someone was looking out for them. People think this will never happen to them but we are a society in denial when it comes to money. The truth is, the number one person looking out for you, needs to be you.

Overlooking or misunderstanding your risk exposure can be financially devastating. However, the solution is simple. An in-depth risk analysis will provide a clear outline of your holdings. Our team breaks down the historical performance of each of your investment positions. This includes their highs and lows, so you can begin to interpret how your investments typically perform in various market conditions. Using this information, you can then make informed decisions regarding whether you are comfortable with the risk those investments carry.

If you don't have a risk analysis of the investment losses within your portfolio, make it your top priority. You have a right to know what could happen before it jeopardizes your financial security and well-being. This is why we focus so heavily on education. You need to have the facts and a clear understanding in order to confidently make decisions that will impact the future reality for both you and your family.

Losses Hurt More Than Gains Help

Let's imagine a scenario where you have $100,000 in investments. It took you a long time to save that $100,000 and it's a lot of money, which you have responsibly set aside for the future. How much would you be willing to lose? Suppose the stock market experiences a decline similar to that of 2000, 2008, or 2020. How much of your $100,000 are you comfortable giving up?

You must measure whether the potential losses of your investments align with what you are willing to lose when a market correction occurs. By its nature, the stock market ebbs and flows. It's not a question of if, but when.

This is merely scratching the surface of why it's so vital that you consider how your holdings are likely to perform based on data. I can't emphasize this enough: the key to success lies in recognizing that losses hurt you more than gains help you.

What does this mean?

Well, let's start with that $100,000 again. If your risk exposure is about 10%, that means a market correction could cause you to lose about $10,000. You'd be left with $90,000. So now, any hope of recovering those losses would require an 11% rate of return. That's right: since you now only have $90,000 invested, you will need an 11% rate of return to recover the 10% loss you just had.

This is why losses will always hurt you more than gains help you. Losses put you in a situation where you need more and more, to get back to where you were. I say it all the time: "No one likes to lose money!" I'd venture to guess you don't either.

Let's take this one step further. The largest market loss for the S&P 500, between 2007 and 2009, was a decline of 50.95%. I doubt anyone could say that's not significant. Just imagine: your $100,000 would have dropped by $50,950, leaving you with a net of $49,050. Can you still retire if that happens?

This is exactly what happened to countless individuals who watched their investments plummet from the high of 2007, down to the low of 2009. This is scary stuff and economic indicators are lining up for this to happen again in the near future. Except now, what would you have to earn the following year to recover from such a tremendous loss of 50.95%? It would take about a 102% rate of return to recover. Is that really going to happen? Not likely!

Take a moment to reflect on how much you lost in 2008. Many people I've met with took even bigger losses between the stock market high of 2007 and its lowest point in 2009. I see average past losses of 55% to 60%.

How can you become more educated on the risk in your portfolio? Analyzing the past losses of your current investments is the best place to start. Have you looked at how the investments you have today faired back to 2000 and 2008?

Perhaps you've heard the disclaimer, past performance is not indicative of future behavior. This statement reflects the fact that yesterday's well-performing investment may not last until tomorrow. Its purpose is to protect brokers from being sued if they lose investors' money. The truth is, stocks and investments which saw sharp declines in the past, are just as susceptible to a similar downturn in the future. Their past behavior will often be a great indicator of what to expect for future market corrections since the risk exposure remains.

Today we are facing very volatile stock market ups and downs with uncertainty for what the next days, weeks, months, or years have in store for us. This creates anxiety and a fear that we will lose all of our money. The "talking heads" of Wall Street say that you need to be in the market to keep up with inflation, but people keep seeing their accounts going down. What are you to do?

We have been operating within such inconsistent financial environments for so long. Isn't it time to take control and demand some consistency in the outcomes of your immediate, future, and retirement savings? For the majority of people, wealth simply doesn't happen overnight. Yet, financial ruin often can. Limit your loss risk and seek consistent returns, over time, if you hope to build wealth.

You can consistently grow your investments to outpace inflation while protecting what you have worked so hard to build. A realistic understanding of your true loss potential will prepare you to ride out future market fluctuations with a level head and realistic expectations.

Recover thousands of dollars and put this wasted money to work for your retirement. Every month you wait is lost wealth.

Get started now with your FREE Wealth Recovery Checklist: www.RetirementByDesignBook.com/checklist

---

Chapter 4

What is a TRUE Comprehensive Financial Planner? Why Do You Want One?

At this point, you are beginning to see how our Wealth by Design team stands apart from other advisors. So, let me ask you, what do you believe a comprehensive financial planner really is? The majority of people think that financial planners are stock brokers and money managers: if you have money in the stock market, a financial planner manages it. While that is one thing they do, they should be doing so much more.

Your comprehensive financial professional should be assisting you with any financial decision you make: from buying a vehicle or purchasing real estate, to selling your business or choosing the banks you want to work with. He or she should know how to manage all types of investments, insurances (life, disability, long-term care, etc.), and other assets. Your advisor should be able to determine the cause and effect of the financial decisions you make today on your end results in years to come and project those dollars out for you to clearly see and understand. He or she should be able to help guide you on the best income strategies for your retirement, whether it is next year or 20 years from now.

Your planning should encompass the care of your family in the event you cannot, cash flow analysis of where your money must go for college planning, retirement income planning, tax strategy planning, estate planning, and so much more. A true comprehensive financial planner can educate, guide, and support you, through every financial decision you face in your entire lifetime.

Our team's focus is uncovering the hidden costs of doing business with Wall Street, banks, government, and other financial institutions you interact with. We start from right where you are now, wherever that may be. You will never be told that you did anything wrong. We ask you thought-provoking questions so that you can be confident about your financial position today, as well as your future financial success for years to come. We work with you to design a customized, well-thought-out plan that you thoroughly understand. We emphasize establishing a comprehensive and coordinated approach that enables you to move confidently in the direction of your goals, dreams, and desires. Our team's priority is making your wish list a reality. The planning and strategies that we create support your unique goals and are in your best interests, not anyone else's.

Many advisors out there could be considered glorified stock brokers or money managers: most concerned with how to invest your current assets on Wall Street. Does your financial planner or advisor have what it takes to get you through the complexity of life's financial decisions? If you don't feel confident, it's time to get that second opinion and receive the type of professional care and guidance you deserve.

Everyone's financial journey is unique. You've worked hard and you've accomplished amazing things. It's time to learn about these overall wealth goals and how you can create the ability to spend that wealth over your lifetime without the fear of running out of money. It's time to benefit from clear advice with recommendations that will focus your efforts and put you on the path to the future of your dreams. Let's outline your future vision and how to accomplish your goals in a way that is simple to understand. You can achieve success based on your ability to be disciplined and consistent in following a well-designed plan to get you there.

You may have already acquired your wealth; now the challenge is to keep as much of it as possible, without others taking it from you unknowingly and unnecessarily. Or, perhaps you still have several years of work ahead of you to get to where you want to be. Regardless of where you currently are in your financial journey, it's important to be disciplined and remain committed to reaping the rewards you deserve and avoid being taken advantage of financially anymore. That's why you are here: to gain a level of knowledge greater than what you have today.

You deserve to have a financial dream team in your corner! This starts with a comprehensive financial planner who makes it easy to understand your financial picture. They should have a working relationship with your tax professional and estate planning attorney to do what it takes to plan for your success. You want all your "money people" talking and strategizing with you every year.

Do you meet with your financial team prior to the end of each year to project what your tax consequences will be for the coming year? Unfortunately, many people overlook this because they are too busy. It's difficult to avoid common tax pitfalls when you fail to plan. Burying your head in the sand and hoping your decisions won't adversely affect your bottom line is not an effective strategy.

If you haven't had proactive planning in the past, don't beat yourself up. You are here now and you are not alone. It's time to make up for the lost time. Educate yourself and put the work in to make sure you achieve the outcome you desire.

Chapter 5

What Is the Number One Investment You Should Make?

We've talked about the dangers in today's financial climate. So, what can you do? How can you protect yourself? You can start by investing in your number one investment.

First of all, what would you say is your best investment? Most people believe, or will tell me, that this is their home. Others believe it's their retirement plan account(s). Let's think about this for a minute. Is your primary residence an asset or liability? Does it produce an income or is there a cost for deferred maintenance? How about your 401(k) or 403(b), company-sponsored retirement contribution plan? Are your retirement plans the all-encompassing answer to your retirement picture? They are only a piece of the puzzle.

Think about what your best investment is...

It's YOU! Without you, your desires and visions for the future do not exist; nothing matters. So, why aren't you investing in yourself?

If you could invest in yourself, knowing that you are the best investment to make, how much would you invest? $1? $5? $10,000? $1,000,000? I sometimes hear, "As much as I possibly can."

Now, the next question is this: if you invest in yourself, how would you choose to spend the money that you invest, and are you worth it? Your children think so; your spouse thinks so; your company thinks so.

Michael Jordan was the first individual who invested in himself in the 1980s. He did so by incorporating himself. Everyone knows who he is; especially his family, who are likely to benefit from his immense estate. He has a net worth of $1.31 billion and has been investing in himself for a long time, asking for as much as he could. However, you do not have to be a professional athlete to invest in yourself.

What is Your Human Economic Value?

How does this fit into what I am talking about? It has to do with determining your Human Economic Value and making the most of it!

Have you ever heard of this term before?

The economic value of an individual's life is the amount calculated from his or her yearly income, the future income leading to retirement, and other variables such as savings and assets. This determines the financial loss a family will suffer in the case of a family member's death. This calculation also helps determine the amount of insurance that a person qualifies to receive.[2]

To put it simply, your HEV represents your earning capacity for the rest of your life. This is why each person we work with is their number one and most important asset. The power of this number comes when you choose to insure your HEV with a well-designed permanent life insurance policy. This enables you to use your money to invest in yourself while establishing the power and control to be able to spend and protect your HEV over your lifetime; all while protecting your family if you prematurely pass away.

For example, suppose you currently earn $125,000 a year and receive a 2% annual increase, on average. You also have about 15 working years left until retirement. Your HEV is approximately $2,204,910.66. This represents the amount of money it would take for your family to maintain the same level of income in the event of your untimely death. This $2,204,910.66 is also the maximum life insurance coverage amount an insurance company would provide, assuming you are approved for coverage. In this case, protecting your HEV with life insurance means your family would receive the money to continue that $125,000 of annual income, increasing by 2% for inflation each year.

Most people want their families to continue to live comfortably when they pass away and are no longer here. In fact, I haven't met anyone who wanted their death to create a difficult financial situation for their loved ones. What will your family's standard of living be once you are gone? Insuring your Human Economic Value enables your family to continue the life you and your spouse have worked hard to build and design together.

You see, life insurance is not meant to make someone rich when you die; it is to continue to live life and raise or provide for your family the way you both envisioned. This is a truly mathematically verified way of determining how much life insurance coverage you need. You're not picking an arbitrary amount of

$50,000, $250,000, or even $1 million. Your HEV represents a large portion of the value you are trying to grow your estate to, so that one day you can retire and live on the same income, adjusted for inflation.

Your HEV can help you determine your target wealth goal for the future. It is how we begin to figure out how much you will need or want to retire. Your HEV is what will fund your goals, dreams, desires, and responsibilities so that life can happen the way you want it to. This is true whether you receive the benefit while living, or if it's paid out once you pass away.

The first question I ask people at this stage is: if you could spend down the life insurance death benefit of your well-designed permanent life insurance policy over your lifetime, how much human economic value, or death benefit, would you like to spend? Some of it? All of it? Or none of it?

The second question I ask is: if you could spend this benefit, tax-free, over your lifetime would that influence your decision even more? Now, it is important to note that the distribution design you decide on during this phase determines on the ability of funds to be paid out tax-free and must be followed without cancellation of the contract. Otherwise, tax consequences may occur. This step of the process can be complicated and is one of the many reasons why our Wealth by Design team is here to help.

Why You Should Avoid Term Insurance

In discussing insurance, please make no mistake; you do not create wealth from simply having a term insurance policy and then letting it expire to end the contract. That is a true loss of wealth. Suppose you had $2 million in the stock market one day but the market crashed the next day, and your account dropped to zero. Would that be a bad day? Of course it would. There is no difference when a $2 million life insurance policy asset leaves your life. Don't let this happen to you.

Term insurance actually equates to being the largest lost opportunity cost for a family. Even so, term policies are frequently purchased and recommended over permanent policies because the insurance company makes the highest profit on selling term insurance. Meanwhile, the likelihood of you dying before age 65 is less than 2%.[3] Why would you want to pay tens of thousands of dollars in premiums over your lifetime to a policy which your heirs will most likely never see a benefit from? What benefit will that expired term policy provide when you need it the most: when you actually die?

Ben Feldman, an American businessman, and author said, ***"The best investment in the world is the one that pays the most when you need it the most, and that's life insurance."*** However, having the right kind of life insurance is just as important as having any at all.

Term insurance is death insurance and no one I have met wants to die young; they want to live long, healthy lives. We always plan for clients to live to age 100 and beyond, which you simply can't do with term insurance. Since it merely acts as a Band-Aid to temporarily fill a gap, the best use of term insurance would be to help you obtain more permanent insurance based on your current insurability. This can be helpful by capitalizing on your present good health because you can be insured and protected today until you obtain permanent insurance, without again having to prove you are healthy a few years down the road.

Now, let me be clear: if you have to have term insurance at younger ages to afford to cover your family, that's still a good decision. However, it is widely known in the finance community that a relatively small percentage of all term insurance policies ever actually pay out. Therefore, the question you need to keep in mind is: where would you like to put your money for the long haul? A sure thing or a maybe?

Let's look at an example of Human Economic Value using fictitious clients, Mr. and Mrs. Wealth By Design.

Mr. Wealth By Design is currently 55 years of age, with a target retirement age of 67 (his age of full retirement for Social Security). Therefore, he expects to have another 12 working years at his annual salary of $175,000.

$175,000 Annual Earnings
x 12 Years
$2,100,000 Human Economic Value

So, Mr. Wealth By Design's human economic value is $2,100,000. To calculate how long this benefit will take care of his spouse and other heirs in the event of his passing, we simply divide the $2,100,000 by $175,000 of annual income, to estimate 12 years.

As you can see, it's not necessarily about making someone rich when you die; it's about providing the economic income they will need to ensure that they have the means to take care of themselves when the event occurs.

So, let's make this conversation a bit more fun and intriguing for Mr. and Mrs. Wealth By Design.

"Mr. and Mrs. Wealth By Design, if you could (figuratively) spend the death benefit of your life insurance contract while you are alive, how much life insurance would you like to have?"

What we usually hear at that point is, "How can you do this?"

Then we ask the next question, "Well, if you could (figuratively) spend the death benefit of your life insurance contract while you are alive, tax-free, how much would you like to have?"

People will tell us, "As much as I can get!"

That is what we show our clients how to do. We can show you, first, how to invest in yourself as your best investment and, secondly, how to spend down your best investment as a tool for a tax-free cash flow strategy.

First and foremost, you have to qualify. This is important because not everyone can. However, if you can't specifically, your spouse, your children, or even your grandchildren possibly can. You can always be the owner of those contracts and still reap the benefits of what we are talking about here.

We meet with individuals all the time who do not need life insurance. However, when we show them what an incredible tool permanent, well-designed whole life insurance can be for those who qualify, people choose to employ it within their portfolio. With the work and heavy lifting on our team's part and a little discipline on our client's part, together we take the necessary steps for self-investment. The best part of this phase of our work with clients is the potential to generate tax-free benefits, if positioned correctly within the current estate tax laws.

Once again, this is why you need permanent coverage and not term insurance. Term insurance starts out relatively cheap when you are younger, but becomes incredibly costly as you age. "No problem," you think, "I won't need it by the time the premiums increase. I will have already worked and saved my money, so I won't need life insurance." That is simply not the case. As you can see in our example above, the time you may really need life insurance is when you are older. This is why term insurance does not fulfill its purpose.

People spend premiums on term life insurance year after year without realizing they are sacrificing an opportunity for long-term wealth creation. They feel protected today, but haven't considered the situation they'll face years down the road. You need a clear understanding of what you currently own, or don't own, to determine how you can fund and protect both your life and your legacy.

Once again, I am talking about you, not a product. This is about investing in you. Wouldn't you prefer to put your hard-earned money where it will grow, build wealth, provide security and be there when you or your family need it, years in the future?

This strategy provides both safety and tax-favorable advantages. There are two common notions I have found to be true for practically everyone: people never like to lose money and they never like to pay more than their fair share of taxes. After all, we work hard for our money, for our families, for the legacy of our estate, and for everything we believe in. No one wants to see it wasted away.

Yet, the reality is, people have more wealth being exposed to taxes than ever before, simply due to poor planning. Thorough planning takes on even greater importance as assets accumulate since there is more to lose. Wealth creation is wonderful; however, paying taxes, year after year, over the course of your life and then again upon your death, is not a favorable scenario.

Ben Franklin once wrote, ***"In this world, nothing can be said to be certain, except death and taxes."*** I genuinely believe that there is so much more we can create to guarantee the financial presence that we all deserve.

Hearing this for the first time, lightbulbs should be going off. The number you are saving for should also be the number you have protection for. Your HEV calculation is that number. This type of meaningful planning is how you protect your dreams for your family and helps you accomplish the amount of money you will need to retire. There will already be a huge emotional loss when you pass away. Why allow it to create financial distress for the people you love?

Recover thousands of dollars and put this wasted money to work for your retirement. Every month you wait is lost wealth.

Get started now with your FREE Wealth Recovery Checklist:
www.RetirementByDesignBook.com/checklist

Chapter 6

Show Me the Money!

Perhaps you're interested in owning and protecting your Human Economic Value, but you're not sure you can afford it. The truth is, you have the money to invest in yourself and take ownership of your HEV, but you don't realize it. It's hiding within your existing personal financial system. We can help you find it and redirect it.

The biggest obstacle standing in many peoples' way is comfortably affording the premium to contribute to their personally designed plan. Nearly everyone wants life insurance; they just don't want to sacrifice their lifestyle to pay for it.

The Wealth by Design team can assist here as well. We never compromise a client's lifestyle to pay for insurance premiums. We take it from everyone else who is trying to take it away from you. You deserve this wealth, not anyone else.

People tell us all the time that they have no money. We always assure them that it's not their problem, it's ours. This is what we do; this is our talent; we help people find the money! This is one of the reasons our approach is so well received and in such demand. If you don't believe me, challenge us. We will find the money you don't think you have.

We find tens of thousands, if not hundreds of thousands, of dollars annually for people who are serious about creating wealth. Hard-earned money, in clients' lives, that they are losing each and every year to financial institutions, banks, the government, and the companies they choose to do business with over the course of their daily life. No one is forced to do this, but many people choose to do so voluntarily, simply out of convenience or because they do not know of a better way.

We can show you how to change this endless cycle within your life and you can reap the massive rewards. But first, you have to ask yourself if you are serious. Do you really want to change? Do you really want to learn? Are you coachable? Are you willing to change the way you do things in your life to welcome much better results? If you are, then we will show you how you can attain far superior outcomes. Understand that this is work, but there is no better use of your time and effort. Our team is ready and waiting to help you.

What is a Lost Opportunity Cost?

A lost opportunity cost is any dollar you have lost due to a fee, have given away unnecessarily or unknowingly (such as taxes, bank fees, or transaction fees), and you can no longer invest to receive profits over time. This cost must be measured and calculated over one's lifetime because you can never recover that dollar or its potential earnings, had you been able to invest it for your financial future. Your lost opportunity costs impact your net worth as a subtraction/loss.

Why do you think we pay these fees without much thought? You work incredibly hard for the money you make; why would you freely give it away? It's all about convenience and time. Or, simply put, bad financial habits. Life is busy, and we are always in a rush. As a result, we make daily decisions to give away our wealth on senseless transactions because we are distracted. It just doesn't seem to be necessary at the time! This is the reality we all face and are guilty of – to some degree.

Now, I'm not saying you shouldn't enjoy life and the things you love. In fact, exactly the opposite: you should be focusing on what you truly love and value the most! Your big dreams and life goals for you and your family should be top of mind with every money decision you make.

It's time to take a conscious pause, reflect on your financial behaviors, and take responsibility for your choices. If you are satisfied with what you are doing and the progress you are making toward your goals, by all means, go ahead and keep doing it. However, you may find that your spending habits don't actually align with the financial dream life you are trying to create. If this is the case, it's time to take action and make meaningful decisions about how you spend your hard-earned money.

This is the most important lesson of the wealth creation process. We show you how to perform a cash flow analysis of all of your expenses and find out what's coming in and what's going out. In this way, we help you understand the lost opportunity costs impacting your ability to accelerate your wealth.

This is the talent of our Wealth by Design team. We help clients to find money in their current financial situation that is being lost to wealth transfers, fees, lost opportunity costs, and more. On average, with a client/couple earning in the neighborhood of

$175,000 worth of income, we will find more than $45,000-$50,000 per year that is going to such areas. We show our clients how to recover these losses and put them into their Wealth Recovery Account, as we will discuss in further detail in the next chapter.

So... Where is the All the Money?

When we meet with people who use credit cards on a regular basis here's an example of how most conversations will go:

Me: "How much are you charging each month on credit cards?"

Client: "Oh, we pay off our credit cards every month."

Me: "Ok, well do you know what you are spending that money on?"

Client: "Well, we put everything on credit cards and pay it off every month."

Me: "That's great, however, how much were you charging per month 5 years ago?"

Client: "Maybe $500-$1,000 per month."

Me: "How much are you regularly spending on our credit cards now?"

Client: "Somewhere in the neighborhood of $3,000 to $4,000, maybe more."

While the numbers vary slightly, the pattern persists: spending on credit cards goes unchecked and increases at a staggering rate. I have these conversations all the time!

It is a perfect example of people doing exactly what these financial institutions want them to do. They entice you with travel points or cash-back rewards but what's really happening is that you are sacrificing your ability to save money in a significant way. Your expenses keep getting bigger, you keep telling yourself "I have to have that" and "I deserve to have this." Overspending and addictive money behaviors are real issues. It's easy to be blinded by denial, but you must acknowledge and take responsibility for your decisions and behaviors if you want to do better.

In the past few years, and especially during the pandemic, the newest addiction has become Amazon. Your dog starts barking when the delivery driver comes up the driveway and rings your doorbell. You figure, "Oh, it must be Amazon."

We are living in an immediate gratification world. Lifestyle creep affects us all. As more money comes in, we find more creative places to spend it. We want convenience, the enjoyment, and we tell ourselves we deserve to indulge. As a result, credit card spending explodes and it's easy to lose track of where all your hard-earned money is going.

Do we really need to have everything we see? More importantly, what will it mean for our future? Is today's latest gadget worth sacrificing the bigger wish list goals we have for our lives and our loved ones?

I'm no saint; I purchase on Amazon and other online shopping sites. The key is being aware of how much you are spending. After all, you owe it to yourself to be honest about what you are doing and why you are doing it.

For example, consider some of the following common fees and expenses which the average American may incur over the course of a year.

Bank Fees: $12 - $24 a month ($144 - $288 per year)

ATM Fees: $3-$5 non-bank withdrawal + $3-$5 bank fee x 3 times a month ($108 - $180 per year)

Venmo Pay Convenience Fees: $200 per month ($2,400 per year)

50% of Target Monthly Purchases: $330 per month ($3,960 per year)

50% of Walmart Monthly Purchases: $250 per month ($3,000 per year)

50% of Dining-Out Purchases: based on our average client's cash flow analysis, this could be approximately $1,200 to $2,500 per month. That's an average of $14,400 to $30,000 per year. It certainly adds up quickly. What if you could recover 50% of this monthly amount? Imagine what could you do with it! Are these restaurants worth giving this much wealth to? For this example, let's aim to recover 50% of the annual cost, so $7,200 - $15,000.

You have to ask yourself: is that a lot of money or is it not that important to me? Lifestyle creep is a dangerous threat so it's important to remember that there is always a cost.

Coffee Shop Habit: $15 a day x 5 days a week = $75 per week ($3,900 per year). Got to get that buzz!

Gym Membership: $30-$100 per month ($360-$1,200 Per Year). Are you using it?

50% of Amazon Purchases: $250 per month ($3,000 per year). Do you really need the latest gadget?

How about all the apps and streaming services you are paying for each month? The average person pays around $200 per month, or $2,400 per year, on Spotify, Netflix, Hulu, YouTube, workout apps, Door Dash, etc. Subscriptions are everywhere, charging you each month whether you use them or not. Do you know how much you are spending on apps and subscriptions every month? You may be shocked when you do a cash flow analysis and find out where your money is going.

Average Credit Card Fee: $350 to $500 per year. Why should you be paying for your money? Is the cashback reward enough to pay the annual fee? What additional transaction charges are you paying because the companies you do business with no longer want to cover the service fees? What about those miles? I will give credit where credit is due, but how many of you have actually used the miles that you have acquired for the use of that credit card? Has it paid off yet?

Average Credit Card Interest: This number can vary greatly, but one thing is for sure, it continues to grow. The average American has a revolving credit card balance of over $7,104 per month, with the cost of this debt in interest around $1,100 per year, per household.[4] Is this happening to you?

What about your tax refund? That creates a lost opportunity cost as well. The average federal tax refund is around $3,100.[5] Is this free money? No way! You earned that money more than a year ago, but you gave the government an interest-free loan to use your money all year. Now, when you finally get your money back, a year later, you take a loss in purchasing power due to inflation.

Total Average Miscellaneous Costs Identified: $30,000 to $40,000 total per year from the above examples.

Is that a lot of money? I think it is. Now, most of it may not seem like much for the cost of doing business, but it sure adds up when you're not looking, or have fallen into a comfortable routine.

Imagine if you had the discipline to commit to a plan and recover those annual costs. What kind of opportunity could you create from those dollars? If you could have invested that $40,000 per year, at an average interest rate of 5% over the next 20 years, it could have grown to $1,388,770.07. This money could be used to achieve the wish list goals for you and your family. If you did not invest it and spent it instead, that represents a lost opportunity cost of $1,388,770.07.

This is a huge amount of wealth lost to these financial entities, governments, and companies you do business with to support your lifestyle. You continue to choose to give away this money to them. Have you stopped to think about why?

It's easy to wrap your daily coffee run into your lifestyle and routine. You may want those credit card rewards and airline points but – at the end of the day – are those companies really giving you something for free for spending your money with them? Or, are they charging you so much more and taking advantage of you with distracting bonus miles and gift cards? Businesses have made it easier than ever to just tap or swipe to pay, use Apple Pay, etc. but why should you pay to use your own money by paying with a credit card?

Living a cash life fosters much more mindfulness surrounding your spending. It's definitely a commitment. However, when you have cash on hand and you need to manage what you spend your money on, I'll bet you know what you spent that $100 bill on. When you pay $100 with that credit card, I'm guessing you hardly have any memory of that purchase.

If you stop to think about it, do you want to continue to give away hundreds of thousands, if not millions, of dollars in your overall lifetime? Or, do you want that money in your control and available for your future? After all, you earned it and you deserve to have it. It's up to you to stop giving your money away and start recovering your wealth today.

Unfortunately, the average consumer often wastes their money on lost opportunity expenses such as these, without much time for thought or reflection. I regularly see even ten times as many fees as this when analyzing a client's cash flow, so we are just scratching the surface with the money I am showing you here in this example.

This is only a small-scale example of a few expenses and what they can represent to our financial future opportunities. Just imagine what your real lost opportunity costs may total. It could be in the hundreds of thousands, if not millions, of dollars over your lifetime.

How much of that lost money would you like to recover? All of it? Part of it? Or none of it? The decision is up to you. Do you know where all your hard-earned money is going? Do you want to continue to make everyone else rich? Or, do you want to recover that lost wealth for yourself?

Again, I am not telling you to not enjoy life, I am simply educating you on how much wealth you sacrifice by not being aware of where all of your money goes. Your wealth does not have to be lost forever. Remember, we want to make different decisions so we get different results in our financial future. We can change the way we look at money, the decisions we make when it comes to money, and our relationship with money right now.

The Wealth by Design team can help you "find the money" and identify the assets and hard-earned money that financial institutions, banks, the government, and your lifestyle are taking away from you in excess. Then, we partner with you to create a plan to recuperate the lost opportunity dollars we have found and put it to work for your future! We accomplish this by establishing your own Wealth Recovery Account™, where you can see your recovered lost opportunity costs build wealth for you.

Again, I ask you: do you want to continue to give away such a tremendous amount of your hard-earned money over the next 20 years or more? When do you plan to do something about all of this lost wealth? When will you take action to thoughtfully align your financial behaviors with recovering and creating meaningful wealth?

Recover thousands of dollars and put this wasted money to work for your retirement. Every month you wait is lost wealth.

Get started now with your
FREE Wealth Recovery Checklist:
www.RetirementByDesignBook.com/checklist

Chapter 7

How Do You Put Your "Found Money" to Work?

One of the most significant steps toward recovering and redirecting the wealth you are giving away is to initiate a **Wealth Recovery Account™**.

Remember all of the expenses you went through in your cash flow analysis to create a budget? Then you "found money," which you now are committed to saving. Every dollar that is no longer going to all those financial entities needs a new place to go. That's the Wealth Recovery Account, and it's the most important bank account you will ever have. It's an incredible tool that will help you dramatically change your personal economic system.

What is a Wealth Recovery Account?

Simply stated, your Wealth Recovery Account (WRA) is a separate checking account that acts as a temporary holding tank for money. This is a bank account at a different bank than you normally bank with today. Why? You will steal from yourself if you see that money is easily accessible. We are our worst enemies. To avoid this, simply set up an automatic transfer from each paycheck to go into your WRA. This is simple using your cash flow analysis work from the previous chapter.

For example, suppose that together, we have found $40,000 per year (or any amount) you can recover from your lost opportunity costs. Fantastic!

Next, you set up an automatic transfer so the found money can be moved to your WRA before you even have a chance to miss it. This is similar to how you pay for benefits like health insurance through your paycheck. If you get paid weekly you would have $769.23 automatically deposited into your WRA each paycheck. If you get paid bi-weekly, you would be transferring $1,538.46 per pay period. If you are paid once a month, you would automatically transfer $3,333.33 per month. This strategy breaks down your total "found money" amount into small amounts and prevents them from being absorbed into your lifestyle. This approach enables you to recover those identified costs that are no longer going out and repurpose them to create your future financial success.

It's YOUR Money – Own It!

Once you have your WRA set up with an automatic transfer from each paycheck, you can begin to implement new strategies and processes to grow that money. Your WRA is a powerful wealth-building recovery strategy because it helps you prioritize your financial security and establish a meaningful structure within your personal financial system.

Here's how:

Protection – All the insurance policies you need to protect what you are working so hard to build.

Savings – Accumulate a "life happens" or emergency expense account. This is for when something breaks, maintenance costs, or other unexpected expenses which could threaten to derail your plans. This liquid money acts as a cushion to help you stay on track toward your larger financial goals.

Growth – Then it's time to grow your investments, real estate, businesses, etc.

Your WRA will hold recovered costs, such as term insurance premiums, interest payments, and dividends. It is also the account from which payments for the new wealth-accumulating programs will be made (i.e., permanent life insurance, municipal bonds, real estate).

The account should be established and labeled properly, as your WRA. When going into a bank, the teller will not know what a WRA or Wealth Recovery Account is. They do not share the same knowledge that I am giving you here. Identifying the purpose of this very important checking account as your Wealth Recovery Account is for you to do; you are declaring your commitment to recapturing your lost wealth by setting up this account.

It's time to create wealth with a purpose. Try not to negotiate with yourself. Find the money, commit to the amount of money you want to recover, and stick to it. Hold yourself accountable and do not steal from yourself. After all, you are the only one who loses.

What Is the Purpose of Your Wealth Recovery Account?

Its primary purpose is to implement and create wealth strategy tools today so that you can live the life you want in the future. It will automatically keep money circulating throughout your financial system, thereby maximizing wealth and benefits.

All inputs to investments will be handled through your WRA. The transfer of money from your protection, savings and growth accounts is also passed to your WRA.

Similarly, the movement of dollars from one account to another within the same component is also passed through this account. This process is called coordination and integration. This may also include adding "new money" to the WRA through regularly scheduled contributions.

The secondary purpose of the WRA is to serve as an exclusive financial register for review purposes. A permanent record of all financial transactions is established for tracking the wealth recovery process. It is a log of transactions providing documentation for present and future tax considerations, such as cost basis and investment expenses.

What Are the Wealth Recovery Account Benefits?

The WRA produces many benefits that include:

1. Complete separation of money: money that you have identified as lost opportunity dollars are now repurposed for your financial

future. Dollars for savings and investments are not commingled with vacation funds, emergency dollars, or spending money.

2. A monthly statement documenting all transactions.

3. A financial case history carried forward from year to year.

4. Repositioning of assets is recorded through the source of the deposit and the ultimate disposition of that deposit.

5. It serves as a clearinghouse for transactions. Your wealth is not misappropriated or spent unknowingly.

6. It provides accountability for reviews, which is often missing in traditional financial planning.

What is Deposited into Your Wealth Recovery Account?

_______ Interest formerly compounded on any investments

_______ Dividends formerly reinvested

_______ Short-term capital gains formerly reinvested

_______ Long-term gains formerly reinvested

_______ Recovered tax savings

_______ Savings from lower deductibles

_______ Recovered term premiums

_______ New money created by bonuses, pay increases, and other additional income

_______ New rent which can be saved

_______ Savings from refinanced debt

_______ Tax refunds

_______ Tax mitigation strategies

_______ Savings from tax (W-2) adjustments

_______ Overpaying of secured debt

_______ Positive cash flow from rental income

_______ Positive cash flow from passive income

_______ Dollars already allocated for life insurance premiums

_______ Investment "pay downs"

_______ Non-matched contributions of retirement accounts

_______ Unused apps, subscriptions, memberships, or other monthly recurring fees

_______ Any "found money" you identify by going over your cash flow spending each quarter

_______ Any excess "lifestyle" expenses that you are consciously going to save now

_______ Other – whatever you can dream up in creating your wealth!

What Will Be Drafted/Paid from Your Wealth Recovery Account?

_______ Life insurance premiums

_______ Disability insurance premiums

_______ Long Term Care insurance premiums

_______ Investment opportunities

    _______ Stocks

    _______ Bonds

    _______ Mutual Funds

    _______ Real Estate

    _______ Investment Property (Airbnb, etc.)

    _______ Collectibles

    _______ Businesses

_______ Life Insurance policy loan repayments

What Your Wealth Recovery Account Is NOT

Your Wealth Recovery Account is not your household account for daily cash flow transactions. It is not for expenses such as auto or homeowners' insurance, mortgage payments, credit card payments, etc. It is NOT another "lifestyle" account.

Your WRA is not for emergencies. You should always have a separate emergency account set up for sudden expenses, such as vehicle repairs. This should be a separate account you maintain that always has a minimum of $2,500 in it.

Your WRA is not a savings account for vacations. A travel account should be set up independently using any "found money" that is identified through your annual review of the "show me the money" cash flow analysis.

Establishing and maintaining your Wealth Recovery Account is a significant first step in getting started on the path to recovering your hard-earned money. It is a powerful tool to recapture dollars that were once lost to the government, financial institutions, banks, etc.

The WRA encourages accountability within your fiscal life, enabling you to create wealth for yourself now and lay the foundation for your dream financial future. This is how you take back the wealth you have been making for everyone else!

Recover thousands of dollars and put this wasted money to work for your retirement. Every month you wait is lost wealth.

Get started now with your
FREE Wealth Recovery Checklist:
www.RetirementByDesignBook.com/checklist

Chapter 8

How Will Inflation Impact Your Money's Future?

Education is such a large part of our approach to the financial planning process because we have seen the incredible impact it makes in the lives of our clients. Being able to make informed financial decisions and feel confident in your chosen path enhances peace of mind, which is truly priceless. The clarity that education provides can remove the burden of financial stress from your shoulders and open up your life to many possibilities you may not have had access to before.

It's time to become educated about your options. As Bob MacDonald, the founder of Life USA Insurance and retired CEO of Allianz, North America states, ***"The primary reason people stop learning is the assumption they know all they need to know."***

Wow! Isn't that a thought-provoking statement? To think that you stop learning because you believe you already know everything you need to know about financial matters, life, or whatever the topic may be.

Bob is right, people fall into this trap of becoming comfortable with what they know. They carry on, ignorant of any blind spots or flaws in the information they've received.

Do you think you know everything you need to know in today's economic environment to survive the financial pitfalls that are happening to people just like you across the country?

In today's busy world, I think we can all agree that there just isn't enough time to know everything as in-depth as we might wish we could. As a result, we may often find ourselves assuming we know enough. However, to consider the effects that knowledge gaps can have on your financial life, whether you are aware of them or not, is rather alarming.

Take inflation, for example. Do you know everything you need to know about how inflation is going to impact your financial plan and your retirement reality in the years to come? Inflation is a silent killer of our finances and a huge variable our country can't seem to control. It often creeps in slowly, over time, so people just kind of accept it. The average inflation rate is typically close to 2% per year.

Recent years have brought increased immediate wealth and government stimulus programs, aiming to avoid a recession or a collapse of the housing market. This has created the highest inflation rate our country has seen in over 40 years. In June of 2022, it hit 9.1%!

The Federal Reserve raises interest rates to try to slow the economy. They worry about being too aggressive and not aggressive enough. The result is that inflation continues to climb, with no end in sight.

One result of this rapid inflation has been an economic boom in real estate. While people love seeing their property values increase, it has created a huge division between those who can afford to own a home (or multiple properties) and those who will never be able to afford to purchase. I am calling this the "Great Divide." This growing separation between the wealthy and the poor has essentially eliminated the middle class as we knew it, prior to the pandemic.

The cost of gas and groceries has been impacted as well. Recently, consumers were paying about 50% more to fuel their vehicles, compared to a year ago. Meat prices at the grocery store have skyrocketed. New and used cars cost over 40% more than before the pandemic. How will the average American continue paying for these increasing costs of goods we can't live without? Are you willing to change your diet from meat to lentils and legumes because you can no longer afford the price of chicken and beef? What choice do you have when you need to feed your family and fuel your vehicle to go to work and earn a living?

I encourage you to read about the hyperinflation which occurred in the 1970s and its impact on all areas of people's lives in the 1980s. There were rapid increases in real estate values at that time too. Everyone thought prices would come back down, but they never really did. The term stagflation grew in use, referring to the rising costs, coupled with slow economic growth and high unemployment. Could we be facing a similar situation in the next decade?

Our team has met with many people who planned to retire out of state in order to enjoy a lower cost of living, but prices have risen everywhere! The rapid increase in real estate values, higher food and fuel prices, as well as supply chain issues, all mean that costs across the country have escalated beyond our imagination.

Do you have hard-working assets, reliable income streams, and enough money saved to outpace inflation? That is the biggest question today. The average retiree only has enough retirement savings to support them for 7 to 11 years, depending on their lifestyle.[6] Is that long enough to keep you financially secure and help you achieve your goals when your retirement stretches over 30 or 40 years? Certainly not!

Let's look at an example:

Imagine you are living on $150,000 a year at the start of retirement. If we adjust for 2% inflation over 20 years, you would need your assets to provide $222,892.11 of gross annual income each year to maintain the same standard of living you have today. That number is shocking!

Are your investments set up in a way that they can do this, and keep increasing to cover that inflation year after year? Are you confident or does this example make you concerned? Suppose your retirement is in 10 years. That $150,000 adjusted for 2% inflation means you would need $182,849.16 of income each year to maintain the same lifestyle you have today. This is how many people run out of money within their investment accounts to "keep up" with inflationary costs. Don't let that be you.

How can you possibly create that kind of income?

That's what we're going to show you! This is a perfect example of how a lack of knowledge or action could prevent you from being able to retire: today, in five years, or maybe ever. Procrastination could force you to go back to work because you don't have enough money to keep pace with inflation. Everyone sees prices going up, but many people don't recognize what this means for their retirement and the income they will need years from now. When you are on a fixed income in retirement, you'll need to make your money stretch to cover all that you need over each month to take care of yourself. What will you be forced to give up?

Many people today don't realize that a little over 80 years ago, hard-working Americans never dreamed of "retirement." Why is that? Life expectancy was only 64½! That's right: Social Security was introduced as a welfare benefit in the 1940s, yet it was never designed to pay long-term benefits because people were expected to die about 2½ years in.

With today's medical technology keeping us alive so much longer, experts say you may have to work well into your 70s or beyond to retire. Isn't that something? Less than a century ago, no one expected to live long enough to retire. Now, society is telling us that we may have to work until we die because we won't have enough money to enjoy a retirement lifestyle for so many years.

It's time for a paradigm shift surrounding retirement. We must have serious conversations and commit to meaningful action to ensure that the wealth we strive to create is inflation-protected. This is the only way our money will last our entire lifetime, regardless of how long we live!

Recover thousands of dollars and put this wasted money to work for your retirement. Every month you wait is lost wealth.

Get started now with your FREE Wealth Recovery Checklist: www.RetirementByDesignBook.com/checklist

---

Chapter 9

Learn How NOT to Run Out of Money in Retirement!

Who do you think is happiest in retirement? Those who are chasing the market OR those who have a guaranteed monthly and annual income each year from their pensions, that continues to increase to keep up with inflation? The majority of people we meet do not like to chase inconsistency or volatility of the market; they love certainty. Uncertainty creates anxiety and who wants visions of their retirement to be consumed by severe anxiety? No one I can think of, and that's the last thing I'd want for anyone, especially our clients or all of you that I am educating.

Retirement should be a time in your life to enjoy and take advantage of certain freedoms, especially with your time, which most people have to sacrifice during their working years to earn a living. You can enjoy more precious moments with your spouse, partner, children, grandchildren, friends, etc. You can explore hobbies you never had time for while you were busy making a living. Perhaps you'll travel to places you've never seen before and make up for a lifetime of memories that you haven't been able to make while working day in and day out.

Most people want to live the "golden life" in retirement: the life they were always promised and told they could have. In fact, I have never met anyone who wants to reduce their income when they retire. Yet, as we've discussed, many retirees will be faced with a significant drop in their income.

Millions of Americans have not saved or planned appropriately throughout their working years. Those who have retirement funds don't have enough money in them. According to research, 56 to 61-year-olds have an average of $163,577 in savings.[7] Isn't this a scary statistic? How long would $163,577 last you in retirement income? Do you think Social Security will be able to satisfy the difference in the income you'll need to get you close to when you were working? Probably not. You may have lived a wonderful lifestyle while you were working, lived life to the fullest, and taken care of your responsibilities. Now, when the day comes that you want to stop working, sacrifices must be made, and reality sets in.

The fundamental analysis that needs to take place is, **"Will my assets and investments be enough to**

generate the same level of income as while working, and enable me to live comfortably for the rest of my life, no matter how long I live?" The answer to this crucial question will determine your success.

Regrettably, for many people, the answer is no; despite working hard and saving for many years, their money simply won't be able to provide the retirement they have dreamed of living. They will either be forced to sacrifice their standard of living in order to try to make their money last longer, or live well for a few years and see their savings wiped out. What happens then? Who will be there to save them? The government? Their children?

Most people have been led to believe they won't need as much money in retirement. Have you given that some thought? Do you believe that is true? You shouldn't if you were paying attention to the previous chapter on inflation.

From my experience, it's far from accurate. Retirees typically spend money on different things vs. their working years but, the fact is, we will all need more money in our retirement years to take care of ourselves. We'll want to travel, spend time with loved ones and enjoy our hobbies. We'll need to fix the roof and afford the rising costs of food, fuel, and medical care. One day soon we may even need a new electric car when that becomes the only option for drivers. Life is getting more expensive every day. If we don't have enough retirement savings to satisfy our income needs, how are we going to live?

The money you are trying to save for retirement acts differently in retirement compared to the years you are earning it. As you're working and earning an income, you don't always need it each month; when you retire, you depend on it!

Following the cyclical nature of the market, retirees often run out of money based on market volatility. This happens because they are forced to take higher distributions to keep up with the demands of increasing costs.

This umbrella of rising costs includes higher prices due to inflation, as we've discussed, but also the growing healthcare costs and medical expenses which consumers are facing today. Technology and medical advances have achieved wonderful things in terms of aging care possibilities but a high price tag comes along with it.

You see, risk variables accumulate as you age. Before you know it, you're not only reeling from market fluctuations but also struggling with the stress of rising medical costs and your growing risk of a major health event. Panic sets in when your assets fail to meet your needs.

Are you worried that this will be you?

What if you could attain the security of knowing that such devastation will not happen to you, regardless of what happens with the markets or increasing expenses? This is the security we specialize in creating, through retirement income distribution planning. Along with protecting your Human Economic Value, you can establish a "permission slip" to act as asset protection and ensure your legacy is always there for your loved ones and estate.

Let's consider an example.

Suppose you have $1 million in an account, from which you can take $21,800 out per year (the Prudent Distribution Method) to sustain your life through your life expectancy. Does that make you feel like a millionaire today? My guess would be, probably not.

Now, let's assume your annual household income before retirement was $175,000. To determine your retirement income, we'll use values based on an average American household.

$36,000 – Social Security, Husband (at 67)
$18,000 – Social Security, Wife
$21,800 – Interest Distributions from 401(k)
$75,800 – Total Annual Income

So, let's think about this for a moment. Even after successfully accumulating $1 million in a qualified retirement account, you are looking at an annual retirement income that is 57.14% less than when you were working. With this in mind, does it come as a surprise that so many people say they can't stop working?

Despite only having their 401(k) accounts to support their retirement, most people are only saving a fraction of what they need, with two-thirds of all Americans failing to contribute to a retirement plan at all.[8] We have a crisis in the distribution and protection phase of retirement planning throughout our country today. People need real help, and many are at a loss for where to turn. Can you afford to live off of 57.14% less than what you are earning today? In the previous example, that equates to living on

$99,200 less of income, every single year for the rest of your life.

Now, let's reimagine a similar example for our clients, Mr. and Mrs. Wealth By Design, only with a few adjustments. Let's suppose they own $2 million of permanent whole life insurance which creates a "permission slip" to spend down more of their assets while they are living. This employs life insurance as more than just a death benefit when one person passes away.

$36,000 – Social Security, Husband (at 67)
$18,000 – Social Security, Wife
$65,000 – Spend Down of 401k Principle & Interest at 4%
$60,000 – Spend Down of Life Ins. Cash Value
$179,000 – Total Annual Income

In this case, our clients can spend down their 401(k) savings over their lifetime because of the financial safety net the permanent life insurance will provide upon either spouse's passing. In addition, permanent life insurance provides a cash value that the clients can spend down, tax-free, when designed properly.

Overall, with a total annual income of $179,000, this example provides a stark contrast to the previous one. Not only do we prevent a devastating drop in income at retirement, but we're actually increasing the retirees' annual income compared to when they were working.

The important point here is, even if Mr. Wealth By Design passes away during this retirement phase of life, there is a residual death benefit for Mrs. Wealth By Design which will continue to provide tax-free income for the rest of her life.

The difference between these two examples exhibits the leverage of thoughtful planning and provides an illustration of how powerful insurance can be. We are merely scratching the surface of the extent to which your *Retirement Income for Life Action Blueprint* can illuminate the key areas of focus and crucial steps required to achieve a dramatic impact on your journey to an ideal and secure future.

What is a Retirement Income for Life Action Blueprint?

As you may expect, the precise path to success and the essential steps to achieving financial security vary with every individual and their unique circumstances. That's why we work with you to develop a Wealth by Design *Retirement Income for Life Action Blueprint*:

a visual model that shows you a set of customized strategies for achieving your unique financial goals. This includes protecting your assets, wealth accumulation strategies, the cause and effect of what these strategies create, tax mitigation strategies, desired income at retirement, as well as financial and estate planning outcomes. We present this as a one-page summary of your current financial picture, identifying strengths, revealing weaknesses, and delivering clear options as a list of direct actions to accomplish your goals.

This blueprint also provides mathematical calculations verifying that there is a more efficient way to accelerate your wealth and accomplish your financial goals. These strategies are designed to create better protection benefits, greater money supply, and improved cash flow efficiency. We provide a projection of your guaranteed income sources in retirement and what you can expect from your investments in the distribution phase of your life. We develop a customized Income for Life Plan based on the strategies presented to you in order to illustrate your potential outcomes, if and when you choose to implement such an approach. We help you achieve improved cash flow to enhance your lifestyle without spending any more than you are currently spending today.

All these areas are based on your goals from your personal wish list. This is key! Everything must be in alignment with your goals! If you have enough money each and every month, can you accomplish all of your goals in retirement and live the life you deserve and want? The answer is YES!

Recover thousands of dollars and put this wasted money to work for your retirement. Every month you wait is lost wealth.

Get started now with your
FREE Wealth Recovery Checklist:
www.RetirementByDesignBook.com/checklist

Chapter 10

It's ALL About the Income!

As we've mentioned, the fear of running out of money is the number one concern for most people at or near retirement. Of course, the question becomes, how do we solve this worry?

You may have noticed that the examples in this book all talk about monthly or annual income. That is because I am here to tell you that Income Is the Solution! When it comes to creating financial security and living life the way you want, it all comes down to income.

Why did you work all those years? Income!

Why don't you think you can retire? Income!

Why do you fear you can't stay retired? Income!

Income supports our needs and wants; it makes our daily life possible and enjoyable. Without it, we are stuck: everything is limited or out of reach. This is where stress and anxiety overtake a life of happiness and peace.

In order to eliminate the fear, you need to know that you won't outlive your income.

Ask yourself: Where will I get my weekly, bi-weekly, and monthly income once I retire and I am responsible for generating my income for the rest of my life? Many people can't answer this, which is exactly why they don't have as good of a plan as they think they do. The answer is guaranteed income. You need a plan to create guaranteed income, not only for you but also for your spouse. This protects both of you, regardless of who dies first.

As we've discussed, life gets more expensive the longer you live. While you're working, you can just earn more money. In retirement, it can mean disaster for your quality of life. Consider what this means for your income planning. If you plan your guaranteed income streams for retirement to satisfy your needs today, you will fail. You'll face a problem because your future needs are going to be more, just based on inflation alone. This does not include additional healthcare, medical expenses, more frequent travel, or any other potential increase in expenses based on your personal wish list.

Many people think they have a plan because they are contributing to a retirement account, paying into Social Security, paying down their mortgage, and maybe even buying real estate. Many business owners assume they can simply sell their business when it's time to retire and they'll be able to live off the profit forever. Once taxes are paid and debts are settled, how long do you suppose that money will be able to support their monthly income needs? Usually not for the rest of their life!

Retirement is a real awakening because our money has to work harder than ever before. Once we are no longer working to earn an income, we need our existing assets and investments to generate our income and support us for the rest of our lives. That's a lot of pressure!

I'm here to tell you the truth and for many people, it's bad news: saving money in a retirement account or planning to sell your business is not creating a plan for your retirement years. It's setting yourself up for failure and frustration.

Let's assume you are saving the maximum annual amount in your 401k, 403b, or other employer-sponsored retirement plans. In 2023, this is $22,500 per year (or $30,000 per year for those over the age of 50). The simple fact is, the amount you can save still won't be able to replace your income today. It won't enable you to maintain your lifestyle or create guaranteed income every year for the rest of your life to replace your income today. That's not even considering inflation. What if you experience a health event? Will you have the money you need to accommodate your new reality? Or will it threaten the financial stability of your retirement? These are serious questions to consider but many people don't understand their options or how to protect themselves. That's why people often push these thoughts aside.

As a financial professional, educator, and thought leader, I bring these conversations to the forefront because I recognize how important they are to people's lives. I've witnessed the dramatic impact that comprehensive planning can have on a family's financial well-being. Unfortunately, I've also seen the devastating effects of poor planning.

Of course, the emphasis here is that you need a well-designed and comprehensive plan. As I've said, trying your best to save money and maximize your retirement contributions is not enough! Is saving and smart money management important? Of course! However, **the real answer to financial security in retirement is INCOME!** Income solves every problem.

Our team recently met with a couple who felt their financial situation was simple. The husband was still working, making a significant amount in his business: over $200,000 per year. They were both receiving Social Security payments, plus positive cash flow from rental properties. In total, they had been averaging a monthly gross income of approximately $24,000.

At the time we met, they had no need for additional money. However, two years prior at age 67, the husband had been declared clinically dead from cardiac arrest. This frightening experience motivated them to come to see us, to make sure the wife would have what she needed if she were forced to live without him.

My initial analysis highlighted the fairly obvious fact that the wife's income would drop dramatically at his passing. His death would mean no more business income and losing her Social Security in order to continue receiving his payments. The wife would continue to receive rental income, though admitting she was not an experienced property manager. She would likely need to hire help: someone to help collect rent, handle unpaid utilities, or increase rents to keep pace with inflation.

They still carried mortgage balances and were considering purchasing more real estate. They also had very little liquid cash in the bank for emergency situations, maintenance expenses, etc. We estimated that, upon his passing, she would bring in gross revenue of approximately $7,500 a month, netting around $6,000 after taxes. I asked her, "Can you live on $7,500 in gross income per month? Can you set aside money for taxes, submit quarterly payments to the government, pay property taxes and health expenses, handle deferred maintenance costs on your real estate, etc. in addition to your daily living expenses?

With no other liquid money to rely on, she'd be living on about $16,500 less, per month, than what she was used to with her husband. Yet, she'd still need to fund most of the same expenses and possibly even hire a property manager to handle their rental properties.

That's an income loss of 68.75%. That's a lot of money to give up each month. That income drop is worse than any market loss or divorce result that our team has seen.

Think about your situation. Could you accomplish everything you do with 68.75% less income? Would you still feel that you could breathe, live comfortably, visit your grandkids, and do everything you hoped to? What if you experienced a significant health event? Research shows that 70% of people aged 65 today will need some form of long-term care services in their lifetime.[9] This could be at-home care or an assisted living facility, but it will be costly either way.

My point is that widows or widowers should not have to face these situations when a spouse passes away. These are topics that should be discussed and planned for in advance. We know life events will happen; it's just a question of when. Planning for possible situations in advance puts you in control. You can think through what you want and make decisions with a clear head. By doing so, you avoid allowing yourself to become a victim of circumstance.

If there were a possibility you and your spouse or partner would suffer from a devastating income loss, wouldn't you want to know about it immediately? Wouldn't you want the chance to make those critical decisions and course correct now to protect your future? This is why procrastination is not an option; it is a death sentence. These are serious conversations that you can't afford to delay. Avoiding difficult or uncomfortable conversations about your money will not make the issues go away. In fact, it will only make them worse.

Clarity is the key. Working through your concerns, getting answers to your questions, and achieving a better understanding of your income picture is the only way to move forward with confidence. Your financial future is too important not to plan ahead.

Choose to be proactive, rather than reactive. Once you experience a dramatic income loss, it will be too late: you may never be able to recover. By making educated financial decisions today, you can avoid the income drop altogether. After all, life is going to happen whether you are prepared or not. Don't you want to know that you did everything in your power to make the most of it?

Recover thousands of dollars and put this wasted money to work for your retirement. Every month you wait is lost wealth.

Get started now with your FREE Wealth Recovery Checklist: www.RetirementByDesignBook.com/checklist

Chapter 11

How do you Solve the Guaranteed Retirement Income Problem?

So far, we've discussed retirement vehicles and investment risk. How to become more educated about your options and how to better prepare yourself by focusing on generating guaranteed income streams that will provide for the rest of your life.

In this chapter, I will introduce you to the term **Private Pension**. A private pension is a strategic financial investment tool that will provide you with a guaranteed, reliable stream of income that you can't outlive! The peace of mind a private pension can provide is hard to beat when it comes to income. If you don't have a pension from your employer, it's time to create that same type of lifetime income with tools available today that serve this purpose.

Let's start by setting up our example.

Consider a couple, ages 65 and 60, who are doing some late-stage retirement planning. Their combined gross annual income while working has been $175,000. They have contributed the maximum amount to their retirement plans at work every year since they turned 50. They have a combined balance of approximately $425,000 in their accounts and will both be eligible for Social Security. Their rental real estate income nets about $2,500 per month, after tax and expenses, for about $30,000 annually. They also have $100,000 sitting in cash for peace of mind to cover emergency expenses and other unexpected costs that pop up.

Due to their experience with a family member, they are aware of how a major health event could impact their retirement and do not feel prepared. One of them had a parent who was in long-term care for more than 10 years. They are concerned about what a similar situation might do to their finances and their ability to pass down a legacy to their children and charitable interests.

Today they net approximately $125,000 after taxes, retirement savings, and health insurance are taken from their paychecks. They spend and enjoy about $10,417 per month.

Do you think this couple will be able to recreate the same amount of net income using the assets they've accumulated and their retirement income streams? Or, will they be forced to take a pay cut?

Let's take a closer look.

Spouse A, age 65

$300,000 Retirement Assets

$2,600/month Social Security

($31,200 gross annual income)

Spouse B, age 60

$225,000 Retirement Assets

$1,800/month Social Security

($21,600 gross annual income)

$2,500/month Rental Income

($30,000 gross annual income)

Now let's see what their guaranteed income sources look like in retirement:

Spouse A

$2,600/month Social Security

($31,200 gross annual income)

Spouse B

$1,800/month Social Security

($21,600 gross annual income)

$2,500/month Rental Income

($30,000 gross annual income)

Total Income

$6,900/month or $82,800 gross annual income

It's important to remember to differentiate between gross vs. net income. Gross refers to the entire amount before any taxes or other deductions are taken. Net is the amount of income you can expect to receive after taxes and other adjustments.

Remember, this couple has been living on a net income of $10,417 per month while they were working. This is the amount they actually received once all taxes, withdrawals, health insurance, and retirement contributions were taken out. A retirement income of $6,900 gross per month will net approximately $5,200 per month, after taxes and expenses. This is $5,217 less spendable money each month. So, this couple is facing a 50% loss of income, if they were to retire right now. Can they do it?

If they retire with $6,900 gross per month, they are going to be forced to make some decisions: Are we willing to change our lifestyle in a dramatic way? Should we continue to work and save more money? Or, should we phase into retirement over several more years until we are more comfortable with less income? These are serious, life-altering questions to consider.

In fact, speaking of life-altering circumstances, the other question we need to examine is what happens if Spouse A passes away before Spouse B? How would that impact Spouse B's income? Would it be the same or drop even more?

Spouse A

$2,600/month Social Security

($31,200 gross annual income)

Spouse B

Social Security Stops and will only receive Spouse A's

$2,500/month Rental Income

($30,000 gross annual income)

Total Income

$5,200/month or $62,400 gross annual income

Is Spouse B in Trouble? I'll let you answer that.

There are many more questions to ask. To start, you may be wondering, "why haven't you addressed the $525,000 of retirement savings? Let's talk about that.

In this example, the couple has a $5,217 loss of income each month. That is $62,604 a year, net of taxes, which they need to make up for in order to continue their current lifestyle. Can it be done with their retirement account savings? How long would $525,000 last, if they withdraw an additional $62,604 net each year to make up the difference? Eight years, maybe? What happens when the money is gone?

So far in our example, we've been outlining the couple's guaranteed income. There's a reason for that: no one wants to find themselves in a situation where they thought they'd have income coming in, but they don't. When the money runs out, the story only gets worse. These are stories we see every day. But, guess what? It doesn't have to be this way.

Remember when I explained that you cannot depend on the market to give you consistency? The market is going to have highs and tremendous lows. Can you count on consistent income from such a volatile account structure? No; you simply cannot.

So, how do we solve the income problem and help the couple in our example retire with confidence? We need to increase the guaranteed maximum joint income over their lives. How do we do that?

We create a **private pension**.

This is where we will be examining the concept of an annuity. Here's what I imagine happens next: you snap to attention and think, "Hold on, stop everything!" Cue the record scratch sound effect. "She said annuity – I'm out."

I completely understand that you may cringe at the word. In fact, I do too.

You may say to me, "Elisabeth, I hate annuities!"

I would say to you, "I do too."

The majority of annuities out there today are terrible: horrific, even. As a result, the word annuity has gotten a bad reputation – and for good reason. However, one small detail far fewer people understand is that about one to two percent of annuities are truly powerful income-generating vehicles! The biggest danger here is not understanding the difference.

You don't want an annuity with high and/or hidden fees, no liquidity, and no ability to leave a legacy for your heirs. You want a particular type of annuity that can replace the missing income when you retire, eliminate the fear of running out of money, and provide the flexibility you deserve.

Let's explore what that looks like.

Pensions vs. Annuities: Love 'Em or Hate 'Em?

What do people love so much about pensions? The guarantee! No speculating, hoping, or stressing about whether you'll have the income you need. You know it will be there and it's yours to live on; to spend as you want or need; to enjoy in return for years of hard work and sacrifices.

Well, guess what? Believe it or not, pensions are annuities. Social Security is an annuity as well. Each provides a guaranteed income source, paying out a specified amount over a person's lifetime, once they retire.

Many traditional pensions also included options to provide for an individual's spouse, in the event he or she outlived the former employee. Upon retiring, the employee would elect whether to reduce the monthly payment amount in order for their spouse to continue receiving income once they die. This is known as a survivor benefit. The options would typically allow for the spouse to receive 75%, 50%, or 25% of the retired employee's monthly pension payment amount.

Guess what? You can create a private pension with the same provision for survivorship income by using the right type of annuity. This **joint life income** is a key benefit for married couples because it will continue to pay out the same amount of income, regardless of who dies first. Therefore, you can protect yourself, and your spouse, against a drop in income and guarantee that your private pension income will not reduce, no matter what happens.

Your private pension can offer another significant income benefit when set up with the right type of annuity. Not only can you guarantee that your income will never decrease, but you can also elect to receive annual cost-of-living increases so that your income actually increases as you age. How about that? **Inflation protection is built right into your guaranteed retirement income stream!** An annual cost-of-living adjustment (COLA) is another benefit older traditional pensions used to offer which has become almost nonexistent today.

It's ironic: People love pensions and hate annuities. Yet, fundamentally, they're the same concept.

Now that we've gone through the similarities between pensions and annuities, there is also a major difference for you to consider. With an employer pension, what happens to the bucket of money that created the pension when both you and your spouse die? Will it go to your children, preferred charities, or other beneficiaries? The answer is no.

This is where a private pension outshines even well-loved traditional pensions: once you and your spouse have both lived long and happy lives, receiving income as you choose, the lump sum of money you started the account with does not die with you. The remaining account balance can go to your children as an inheritance, other beneficiaries, or your choice of charitable causes.

Talk about making the most of your hard-earned money!

Now, let's return to the couple in our example and see what their $525,000 of retirement savings can do when used to create a private pension.

As we know, this couple wants to retire right now. We want to make sure that they can live comfortably and stay retired successfully. Let's suppose the couple opts to protect $400,000 of their retirement savings and use it to create a private pension. Meanwhile, we set aside the additional $125,000 in a managed money account aligned with the couple's stated risk tolerance.

They plan to retire and begin taking income immediately. The income table provided by their annuity shows this would create about $18,000 of additional guaranteed income for the rest of their lives. They elect to structure their income payments so they receive a cost-of-living increase each year to keep up with inflation as time passes.

Let's look at the numbers and see how this impacts the couple's income gap.

Spouse A

$2,600/month Social Security

($31,200 gross annual income)

Spouse B

$1,800/month Social Security

($21,600 gross annual income)

$2,500/month Rental Income

($30,000 gross annual income)

$1,500/month Private Pension Joint Income

($18,000 gross annual income)

Total Income

$8,400/month or $100,800 Gross Annual Income

We'll estimate this could net them approximately $7,080.17 per month or $84,962 each year to spend.

Is that a little better? Definitely. It's not exactly what they were living on while working, but it's far better than the retirement they had originally prepared for.

With additional cash flow, these clients could apply and implement a long-term care plan. If you recall, they were concerned about avoiding a similar situation to what they had seen another family member go through. This coverage gave them peace of mind, knowing they had protection against an unexpected health event derailing their finances. Neither spouse wanted to sacrifice all of their assets to be able to afford care if they were in need. They knew the money would be there for them, enabling them to focus on other things.

Think of it this way: there is a tool for everything. Regardless of what it's called, if it's the best tool available, you should use it.

There is so much at stake: your future depends on these financial projections and calculations. That's why, even if you think you have a plan, it's critically important to verify it with a comprehensive financial planning professional specializing in retirement income distribution planning.

Recover thousands of dollars and put this wasted money to work for your retirement. Every month you wait is lost wealth.

Get started now with your FREE Wealth Recovery Checklist: www.RetirementByDesignBook.com/checklist

---

Chapter 12

How do you Plan Retirement Income to Last a Lifetime?

With so much of the financial industry focused on wealth accumulation and increasing managed money in the market, many people fail to realize that the distribution income phase can be the most complicated phase of your lifetime. Retirees are no longer working; now it's up to their assets to produce the income needed to support their lengthy retirement ahead.

The Social Security Administration estimates about one of every four 65-year-olds today will live past age 90, with one of every 10 living beyond age 95.[10] This means that, realistically, the traditional financial planning methods of those who have planned for a 20-year retirement have resulted in a huge population who have planned for failure. Why? People are living far longer than they ever dreamed of, due to a combination of factors including longer life expectancy rates, advanced medicine, and improved health technology, as well as many people simply taking better overall care of themselves than in the past.

I remember writing the first edition of Wealth by Design; I worked on the book while traveling to New York to celebrate my grandmother's 100th birthday. She never dreamed of living to age 100, yet there she was, celebrating over 45 years in retirement. Could that be you one day, too?

As of just recently, I'm proud to say I'm now a grandmother myself. I'm already taking the steps to plan for both my own lengthy retirement, as well the future for my beautiful granddaughter, Avery. I want to be able to enjoy what the future holds for my family. I know you do too.

We are living in an era where you could be spending more in retirement than during the years that you worked. Do your accumulated assets have what it takes to make this happen? Do they have the power to generate your income in retirement for the next 20 to 40 years or more? As a society, we face a longevity problem ahead of us and we, as individuals, need to make sure that our income will sustain us no matter what.

My goal is to help you understand what increasing longevity means for how we need to plan, if we genuinely want to build the best life possible for ourselves and our families. It all circles back to the fact that you are the one who is responsible for your family's financial security: today, tomorrow, and even once you pass away. If you don't address it now, while you're here, there will be no one to do it once you're gone. At that point, it will be far too late, and your family will be left with the consequences. It's human nature that we do not like to think about these things, but don't you think it's important to talk about them before they happen?

I recently read an article that states the average widow in the United States is age 59. This means that a widow or widower could live another 30 to 40+ years in retirement. You could be living with a financial situation based on decisions you and your partner made together, but they are no longer here.

The article also stated that when couples are planning their financial lives, in the majority of relationships, the financial decisions are largely made by the husband. Only 3% of married women drive the financial conversations for their household.[11] This is drastic and needs more attention. I am passionate about making sure that both spouses or partners, and all parties involved, know what is going on in their financial lives. In every decision, all parties should be on board. An inclusive approach is crucial due to the cause and effect of every financial decision. Not only are parties' immediate lives affected, but there are also lasting repercussions once one person passes away.

The Social Security Dilemma

I've mentioned that depending on Social Security to provide the income you need in retirement is not going to work. Nevertheless, it still provides an income stream that you can factor into your overall retirement picture.

Imagine you're excited about becoming eligible to receive Social Security at age 62. You can't wait to start receiving this money each month. But then you hear everyone telling you to wait until your full retirement age at 67, or even 70. You've worked hard your entire life, making your mandatory contribution to the Social Security system all those years you worked. In some cases, you may have contributed more to Social Security each year than you paid in federal or state income taxes.

As you've seen in some of our examples, when one spouse dies, the survivor will only receive the higher of the two Social Security payments. The smaller Social Security payment will stop. That doesn't sound like an investment you can pass down to the next generation or the charities you love.

My husband and I have had conversations about this subject. He told me he doesn't believe it's fair for that earned benefit to disappear if one spouse dies. I agree with him; most people our team meets feel the same way.

Case Study: How to Fill an Asset Gap

Let's consider a case study to further explore the powerful impact which prudent income planning can have on your overall retirement picture. This example brings together some of the topics we've already covered in order to illustrate a more comprehensive financial plan. We'll discuss using a private pension to address what we call an **Asset Gap** and show you how an individual's HEV can help to satisfy the needs determined by their **Asset Protection Calculation**.

An average couple, getting ready to retire, was introduced to our team through existing clients. In this case, the couple wanted a second opinion from us to see if their current retirement plan was as strong as they believed it would be. So, we happily took a look at their situation.

Both the husband and wife were aged 65 and ready to retire. He worked for a company that would pay him a pension of $60,000 per year, and upon retirement, he could receive Social Security payments of $2,400 per month, for a total of $28,000 per year. Or, if he waited to collect Social Security until his full retirement age of 66.4, he would receive $2,600 per month or $31,200 per year. He was determined to retire as soon as possible, so we ran the projections for him to begin taking Social Security at age 65.

His wife also had a small pension from working for a company for many years, although it was not as much as her husband's. It was going to pay her about $9,000 per year. She was also eligible for Social Security at age 65 for a reduced benefit of $1,100 per month, or $13,200 per year. She knew that she would not have a large pension when she retired, and had saved over $250,000 in a 401(k) throughout her working years. So, here is what their existing plan looked like.

$60,000 – Husband's Pension
$28,000 – Husband's Social Security
$9,000 – Wife's Pension
$13,200 – Wife's Social Security
$110,200 – Total Annual Income

Their annual income, while both of them were working, was in the neighborhood of $145,000. Therefore, they knew they would be taking a pay cut of about $35,000 when they retired, which they both felt they could handle. However, it became clear that they failed to take several other factors into consideration when I began asking some important questions:

1. How comfortable does it feel to live off of $35,000 less in income per year?
2. What happens to your household income if one spouse passes away at age 70? Age 75? Age 80? What if the other spouse passes away first?

For this couple, with their existing plan, here is what her survivorship income would look like if he passed away.

$30,000 – Husband's Pension (Drops by ½)
$28,000 – Keep Husband's Social Security

$9,000 – Wife's Pension
$0 – Lose Wife's Social Security
$67,000 – Total Annual Income

Her annual income drops by $43,200. That's a 39.2% loss of income per year, regardless of how the market or economy is performing. They had already reduced their income by $35,000 upon retiring, and now the wife would be left with even less! This was something they had not even considered.

From what I know to be true for couples today, most have household bills usually based on the total a family earns, not just what half of the income coming in can afford to pay. Not everyone's house is paid off, and many may carry mortgage debt well into their retirement years. Bills for property taxes and insurance costs continue even after a mortgage is paid off.

If a long-term care event occurs in this couple's future, could it affect their life savings and assets? Absolutely. If you can imagine yourself as the survivor here, could you live on an annual pay cut of about $78,000 less than what you were used to living on while you were working? I haven't met anyone who thought they could.

We call this an income or **Asset Gap**: an individual doesn't have enough assets to fill the gap to make up for the income they will lose if a spouse predeceases them.

You may be wondering, "Can this be avoided?" Yes! Not only can this be avoided, but doing so is part of our team's primary focus, right from the start, when we have the privilege to be a part of the retirement planning process with clients and their families. I don't want you to be faced with a significant asset gap or suffer from that kind of predicament, and I know that you don't, either. That's why we show you how to find solutions to correct and prevent this dire problem.

If you recall, the wife had a 401(k) worth $250,000 as she reached retirement. However, the wife was a bit more conservative and wanted to protect the hard-earned money she had saved in her 401(k). She wanted to protect it from loss if there was a market correction, but she also wanted to take advantage of the market going up: the best of both worlds.

At the same time, she needed to establish an income stream to supplement her existing pension. Essentially, she needed to create her own private pension out of this money and have a guaranteed income source throughout retirement, regardless of market fluctuation.

To accomplish her goals, she allocated this portion of her money to a fixed-indexed annuity offering all the possibilities mentioned above. In addition, she was unrestricted in her situation and enjoyed the flexibility of deferring withdrawals until she was ready to take income from her account. How tremendous is that?

So, if she wanted to take income immediately, she could have taken $11,700 per year as a guaranteed income for the rest of her life. However, she didn't need income immediately, so we could position her to have her principal grow until age 70 and begin to take withdrawals at that time. Thus, if her $250,000 grew at an average amount of 6% per year, she would have $334,556, and the guaranteed income for life would be an estimated payment of $16,728 per year.

That is $5,028 more per year for as long as she lives, equivalent to 43% more income just five years later. The considerable increase caused by deferring her income payments can help fill some of the gaps she will face one day.

Now, using this strategy, look at what her survivorship income would be if her husband respectfully passes away at age 70.

$30,000 – Husband's Pension (Drops by ½)
$28,000 – Keep Husband's Social Security
$9,000 – Wife's Pension
$0 – Lose Wife's Social Security
$16,728 – Wife's Protected 401(k)
$83,728 – Total Annual Income

Is that a little better than $67,000? Absolutely.

Not everything is fixed yet, but their situation has certainly improved. Now let's use an Asset Protection Calculation to determine what is still missing. First, we find the difference between their total combined annual income and her new estimated survivorship income to determine the remaining annual income shortfall.

$110,200 Income (While Both Living)
- $83,728 Improved Income
$26,472 Deficit per Year

Next, we take the $26,472 per year and multiply it by their combined life expectancy of age 91, since there is a 50% chance one of them will reach age 91. This calculation illustrates the Asset Gap.

$26,472 Deficit
x 26 Years
$688,272 Asset Gap

This is the value needed to fill the Asset Gap in the event that he dies before her and she lives to age 91.

If we look at it in another way, an asset in the amount of $688,272 divided over 26 years would give her $26,472 per year to make her survivorship income whole. Since they do not currently have such an asset, it needs to be created. This would enable her to continue to live comfortably and avoid creating a financial burden for her, as the person left behind. Ultimately, this is successfully achieving what they both worked so hard for throughout their lives together.

One way they can accomplish this goal is by using discounted dollars to purchase a well-designed, permanent life insurance policy for the calculated amount. Using this strategy simply replaces the asset which doesn't tangibly exist and fills that gap. When it comes to setting up a well-designed permanent whole life insurance policy, now you can understand why it is important to know your **Asset Gap**. This will replace what the wife is missing and grant her a sense of financial security in the event of his passing.

In this case, our team performed a cash flow analysis and was able to fund the life insurance premiums with money identified on their **Found Money Report**. Most significantly, if you recall, this does not impact their lifestyle or additional spending.

With this solution implemented, the couple's final chosen scenario looked like this, in the event of the husband passing away prior to the wife.

$30,000 – Husband's Pension (Drops by ½)
$28,000 – Keep Husband's Social Security
$9,000 – Wife's Pension
$0 – Lose Wife's Social Security
$16,728 – Wife's Protected 401(k)
$26,472 – Husband's Life Ins. Proceeds Create this Income Each Year
$110,200 – Total Annual Income

No matter what, they will always have the same income, regardless of their ages, plus any additional cost-of-living adjustments provided by Social Security increases. Wouldn't you like to have that financial security in your life?

It's clear to see the dramatic effect the use of a comprehensive illustration such as a **Lifetime Retirement Income Blueprint** can have in creating a thorough financial plan. Not only does it enable you to confidently make critical decisions that can influence the rest of your life, but it makes the process straightforward and minimizes anxiety since you can clearly and immediately see their impact.

Recover thousands of dollars and put this wasted money to work for your retirement. Every month you wait is lost wealth.

Get started now with your FREE Wealth Recovery Checklist: www.RetirementByDesignBook.com/checklist

---

Chapter 13

Who Is Holding You Accountable?

Now you understand the power behind designing your own unique retirement income strategy. Your financial future is too important to leave up to chance. You need a roadmap to achieve peace of mind and security within the retirement you desire.

As you can see, achieving an abundant retirement is truly *by design.*

Our Wealth by Design team works to support you on your personalized path to success. Even the greatest intentions and most carefully made plans can be doomed to fail if there's no accountability standard. The last thing we want to see happen is for all the time, energy, and effort you've invested into changing the direction of your financial future to go to waste. We arrange private coaching sessions and monthly, quarterly, and annual review meetings to ensure you stay on track. This is another way we set ourselves apart and raise the expectations for our clients beyond that of other financial professionals.

The truth is, there is no one particular product that does anything magical on its own. Effective planning is all about how you strategically orchestrate everything to work together. There is, however, a mathematical science behind every recommendation, and no individual, couple, family, or business is ever the same. Thus, every recommendation or strategy we help you employ is unique.

Bob MacDonald says, ***"Success comes down to doing simple things and simply doing them."*** The acceleration of your financial success begins with the implementation of all of your decisions. When put into practice, this is nothing short of a complete transformation from the person you were before and how you thought. You will begin to witness the profound difference you are capable of making in your life and your future.

The key is: you must take action!

Procrastination is one of your toughest enemies. Right now, you may be working and thinking retirement is so far off. It's natural to put off what's not right in front of us. However, 70% of retirees say they wish they had started planning for retirement sooner.[12] Don't find yourself living with that same regret 5, 10, or 20 years from now.

People tell our team all the time, "I'm not ready to think about retirement." Yet, everyone we meet with admits they want to have options, pay fewer taxes, and have control over their income.

More than ever, people are looking for the freedom to spend their time how and where they wish. For some people, that means living a "semi-retired" lifestyle and choosing when they work. For others, it means quitting their 9-5 job and starting a business they're passionate about.

Whatever you're looking for in your life, an informed financial and retirement plan is crucial to making it a reality. Not only that, but the sooner you get started, the more possibilities you can create! So, no matter what stage of life you're in, it's time to start prioritizing your relationship with money and designing your ideal retirement.

The truth is, retirement planning is not about planning for one day, far off in the future; it's making informed decisions all along the way, to live life how you wish you live it. I don't need to tell you that the years roll by quickly. My team and I believe in helping you to accomplish all that you've envisioned your retirement to be. We want you to understand that by taking steps today, you can protect against the worry of tomorrow.

Where do you want your financial future to lead?

That's up to you to decide.

The actions you take today will determine the lifestyle you live tomorrow. Your commitment and the sacrifices you make now will pay off in the years to come.

So, what do you do?

Start by accepting that planning is 100% your responsibility. No one else is going to do it for you. You need to consider everything you have at stake and get serious about implementing a plan.

There are so many factors in our lives that are beyond our control that it is crucial to take command of what you can. You want to be equipped to face as many unknowns in your future as possible, while continuing to live your best life today.

It's not necessarily about trying to get ahead in the traditional way; it's about getting ahead by being educated the *right* way.

Our team acts as a guide to help you navigate as efficiently and mindfully as possible. We strive to make the planning process highly logical and protect you, your loved ones, and your estate over time, into longevity.

So, are you ready to make a change? If you are ready to take the next best step in your life, put your dreams into action and commit to one-on-one coaching with me or one of the advisors from our Wealth by Design team.

You deserve better, and you know you do, so stop the madness! Reflect upon all the money you have worked so hard for, on top of all the sacrifices you have made over your lifetime. Consider the time spent away from your spouse, children, and extended family. Honestly, stop and think. You deserve this! What do you want for your life? Now? Five years from now? Ten years from now? What do you envision for your legacy, honestly?

I hope this book will inspire you to take action. Remember, procrastination is not an option: it's planning for failure. That's why it is time to schedule the wealth creation coaching call that will change your life.

Making the commitment necessary to achieve your destiny is all up to you. Our team can show you how to make it happen.

Are you ready to take the action required to take control of your life and get on the right track? You only have one life, and it is time to take massive action to accomplish your true purpose.

Will you do it, or are you just going to talk about it?

It's time to take control of your financial destiny by scheduling your one-on-one Wealth Creation Coaching Appointment with Elisabeth and the Wealth by Design Team of Advisors.

Visit www.wealthbydesignbook.com/free-wealth-discovery-call

References

1 – Meyers, Josh. "New Report Finds Almost 80% of Active Fund Managers Are Falling Behind the Major Indexes." CNBC, March 27, 2022. www.cnbc.com/2022/03/27/new-report-finds-almost-80percent-of-active-fund-managers-are-falling-behind.html

2 – Insuranceopedia Inc. "Economic Value of an Individual Life." March 28, 2017. www.insuranceopedia.com/definition/1669/economic-value-of-an-individual-life-evoil

3 – Social Security Administration. "Period Life Table, 2014" Actuarial Life Table. December 12, 2017. www.ssa.gov/OACT/STATS/table4c6.html

4 – Issa, Erin El. "2021 American Household Credit Card Debt Study." Nerdwallet Harris Poll. January 11, 2022.

5 – Moy, Edmund. "What's the Average Tax Refund and How Are People Using Theirs?" April 6, 2022. U.S. Money Reserve. www.usmoneyreserve.com/news/executive-insights/average-tax-refund/

6 – Josephson, Amelia. "Average Retirement Savings: How Do You Compare?" Smart Asset. September 8, 2022. http://smartasset.com/retirement/average-retirement-savings-are-you-normal

7 – Parker, Tim. "The Average 401(k) Balance By Age." Investopedia. August 17, 2022. www.investopedia.com/articles/personal-finance/010616/whats-average-401k-balance-age.asp

8 – Bhattarai, Abha. "Two-Thirds of Americans Aren't Using This Easy Way to Save for Retirement" The Washington Post, February 22,2017.

www.washingtonpost.com/news/get-there/wp/2017/02/22/two-in-three-americans-will-never-retire-at-this-rate/?utm_term=.14f4c44c9164

9 – U.S. Department of Health and Human Services. "How Much Care Will You Need?" February, 18, 2020. https://acl.gov/ltc/basic-needs/how-much-care-will-you-need

10 – Social Security Administration. Calculators: Life Expectancy. December 18, 2017. www.ssa.gov/planners/lifeexpectancy.html

11 – Dickler, Jessica. "How to Prepare for Being 'Suddenly Single'" CNBC, September 5, 2017. www.cnbc.com/2017/09/05/how-to-prepare-for-being-suddenly-single.html

12 – Reinicke, Carmen. "70% of Retirees Would Tell Their Younger Selves to Start Saving Earlier." CNBC, August 25, 2022. www.cnbc.com/2022/06/25/most-retirees-wish-they-started-saving-for-retirement-earlier.html

About the Author

Elisabeth Dawson

Finance is in My Blood

Helping people with money is in my blood. My story begins with the longest most stressful month of my life in 1998, when my second child, Trevor, was born with severe complications and confined to the NICU. My whole life was about to change.

Suddenly I was facing the need for a new career to have the time flexibility I needed to care for my son. I thought I'd be in retail my entire life, but I needed to transition away from the very demanding and successful career I had as a fashion buyer for Nordstrom.

So, in 1998, I ventured out looking for what felt like a whole new life.

I had no idea what I wanted to do next.

A friend watched my son so I could interview with the GM of a local branch of MetLife.

I almost didn't take the interview because, growing up, two things were off-limits:

Any talk about death or dying.

And my mother's purse!

My mother was from the "old country," an immigrant from Vienna who lived through WWII. For her, conversations about death and money were secretive and fearful.

If you spoke about money, you'd be accused of wanting something when she died. And under NO circumstance... would you ever go into Mother's purse! Never. You might get your hand cut off.

Financial planning was in direct conflict with the two things that were taboo in my family!
A job where you talk about money and death? Not in my family!

But I took the interview, and I loved it.

I felt I was born to help people with life's most difficult subject: money!

I decided to go back to school at night to become licensed.
I was 28 years old.

When I told my parents, they were my toughest critics.

But then something wonderful happened.

At the same time, my father desired to retire early from the government at 55.

As a test of the value of a financial planner, I made an appointment for my parents with my newfound mentor in the industry.

So taboo were the subjects of money and death that my parents disallowed me from attending with them. So, I waited nervously outside the closed office.

"Dear God," I prayed, "If I am meant to be a financial advisor, please show me a sign. Show me even my parents can approve of it."

When my parents emerged, they were visibly happy.

My mom was ecstatic and my dad was thrilled that he could retire.

Mom had always been my toughest critic, and her endorsement was the sign from God I needed to move into the best industry in the world, financial services, with my full commitment.

Since then, I've been blessed to have great mentors who helped me fast-track my career in many ways. But more deeply, I knew I was a woman in a profession full of men, and to succeed, I'd have to be the best. I've always worked extra hard and, because of my children, failure was never an option.

Today I am grateful to be in the top 1% of successful financial advisors in our country. I couldn't have accomplished this without our team - they are incredible.

I found my mission, my passion and my purpose when I found my place in the financial services industry. I'm in my dream job.

There is one moment I'll never forget. It took place just 7 months before my mother passed away.

At a client appreciation dinner, my mother surprised me with an unexpected toast.

"Elisabeth, your grandfather would be very proud of you."

My grandfather was a minister. I didn't know why she was bringing him up.

"I would hope my grandfather would be proud of me, but why?" I asked.

"Your grandfather was the Minister of Finance for Vienna, Austria before WWII."

I was stunned! Growing up, I thought he was a *church* minister.

That unexpected toast privately confirmed something I've felt since my first interview at MetLife. I was born to be a financial advisor - it's in my blood!

P.S. My son Trevor is doing amazing today! He is thriving. We raised him to be incredibly adaptive to his health, and he lives his life like he never had any health concerns. Trevor is an amazing young man. He graduated from college in 3 short years and started his career in real estate as a loan officer. His sister Nicolette is equally amazing. She's definitely the smartest one in the family! Mama is very proud of them both.

- Elisabeth

Elisabeth Dawson is the founder of Copia Wealth Management & Insurance Services, Copia Wealth Management Advisors, Inc., Elisabeth Dawson, Inc., and Wealth by Design. She is an entrepreneur, author, financial coach, certified money coach, comprehensive financial planner, fiduciary, friend, wife, mother, and a new grandmother.

Copia Wealth Management & Insurance Services, as well as Copia Wealth Management Advisors, Inc. are organizations that provide financial and insurance advice with education to help clients achieve their desired wealth goals. Her organization's macroeconomic approach begins with a comprehensive evaluation of a client's "wish list" and financial engineering strategies to achieve successful results with minimized risk.

Unlike other traditional financial planning firms, Copia Wealth Management & Insurance Services and Copia Wealth Management Advisors, Inc. with Elisabeth as President and CEO, educates and counsels her clients through every financial task and decision in their lives.

Elisabeth specializes in working with entrepreneurs, small businesses, individuals, couples, families, and multi-generational legacy families. Elisabeth's financial areas of expertise include life, disability and long-term care insurance, various investment strategies, retirement income planning and protection, tax mitigation strategies, wealth accumulation, and distribution planning strategies to last throughout the growing longevity we are facing today.

With more than 24 years of experience, Elisabeth is more passionate than ever about helping as many people as possible to achieve the dream of their own ideal future and exceed their expectations for a financially successful life journey and a secure retirement.

Made in the USA
Middletown, DE
19 May 2023

30946546R00086